User's Guide and Reference to Ash3d—A Three-Dimensional Model for Eulerian Atmospheric Tephra Transport and Deposition

By Larry G. Mastin, Michael J. Randall, Hans F. Schwaiger, and Roger P. Denlinger

Open-File Report 2013–1122

U.S. Department of the Interior
U.S. Geological Survey

U.S. Department of the Interior

SALLY JEWELL, Secretary

U.S. Geological Survey

Suzette M. Kimball, Acting Director

U.S. Geological Survey, Reston, Virginia: 2013

For more information on the USGS—the Federal source for science about the Earth, its natural and living resources, natural hazards, and the environment—visit http://www.usgs.gov or call 1–888–ASK–USGS

For an overview of USGS information products, including maps, imagery, and publications, visit http://www.usgs.gov/pubprod

Suggested citation:
Mastin, L.G., Randall, M.J., Schwaiger, H.F., and Denlinger, R.P., 2013, User's guide and reference to Ash3d—A three-dimensional model for Eulerian atmospheric tephra transport and deposition: U.S. Geological Survey Open-File Report 2013–1122, 48 p., http://pubs.usgs.gov/of/2013/1122/.

Contents

Figures

Tables

Conversion Factors

SI to Inch/Pound

Multiply	By	To obtain
Length		
millimeter (mm)	0.03937	inch (in)
meter (m)	3.281	foot (ft)
meter (m)	1.094	yard (yd)
kilometer (km)	0.6214	mile (mi)
kilometer (km)	0.5400	mile, nautical (nmi)
Flow rate		
meter per second ($m\ s^{-1}$)	3.281	foot per second ($ft\ s^{-1}$)
Pressure		
kilopascal (kPa)	0.009869	atmosphere, standard (atm)
kilopascal (kPa)	0.01	bar
kilopascal (kPa)	0.2961	inch of mercury at 60°F (in Hg)
kilopascal (kPa)	0.1450	pound-force per inch ($lbf\ in^{-1}$)
kilopascal (kPa)	20.88	pound per square foot ($lb\ ft^{-2}$)
kilopascal (kPa)	0.1450	pound per square inch ($lb\ ft^{-2}$)
Density		
kilogram per cubic meter ($kg\ m^{-3}$)	0.06242	pound per cubic foot ($lb\ ft^{-3}$)

User's Guide and Reference to Ash3d—A Three-Dimensional Model for Eulerian Atmospheric Tephra Transport and Deposition

By Larry G. Mastin, Michael J. Randall, Hans F. Schwaiger, and Roger P. Denlinger

Abstract

Ash3d is a three-dimensional Eulerian atmospheric model for tephra transport, dispersal, and deposition, written by the authors to study and forecast hazards of volcanic ash clouds and tephra fall. In this report, we explain how to set up simulations using both a web interface and an ASCII input file, and how to view and interpret model output. We also summarize the architecture of the model and some of its properties.

Introduction

Atmospheric dispersal of volcanic ash represents the most widespread of volcanic hazards and the hazard with the greatest potential for economic impact. The possible economic effects of ash distribution were demonstrated during the 2010 eruption of Eyjafjallajökull volcano in Iceland, when flight cancellations and delays throughout Europe caused billions of dollars in economic loss to airlines and travelers (Harris and others, 2012). This event also demonstrated that potential volcanic hazards are not limited to areas near the volcano. For example, flight cancellations and delays during the 2011 eruption of Puyahue/Cordon Caulle in Chile extended halfway around the world to Australia and New Zealand.

The most effective way to reduce risk from dispersed volcanic ash is by forecasting where it will go and what areas it will affect. Modern numerical weather prediction (NWP) models now enable us to routinely forecast ash movement in a three-dimensional, time-changing wind field. Modern computer power gives us the ability to forecast where ash will go, and what areas it will affect, within minutes during eruptions.

In this report, we describe how to use our model for atmospheric transport, dispersal, and deposition of tephra. The model, called Ash3d, is an Eulerian model that uses wind fields from NWP models to calculate tephra transport. Model results have been compared with observations from several eruptions thus far. Ash3d provides a variety of output that can be used in research and operational situations. A companion paper (Schwaiger and others, 2012) describes the model physics in detail. This paper describes the model's setup and use and is intended for volcanologists with no expectation of special knowledge in numerical methods or modeling. We begin with a brief overview of Ash3d, explain how to set up simulations using a simplified web interface, and then describe simulations using an ASCII input file and standard Linux utilities. Ash3d is still in development, hence its capabilities and documentation are likely to be revised in coming years.

Model Overview

Ash3d models the transport of volcanic ash by dividing the atmosphere into a three-dimensional grid of cells (fig. 1) and calculating the flow of mass through cell walls. At the beginning of a simulated eruption, tephra is injected at a constant rate into the column of cells above the volcano (fig. 1c). Using a 3-D time-dependent wind field imported from a numerical weather prediction model, downwind advection and diffusion of ash is numerically calculated with a diffusion rate determined by a user-specified diffusivity. Individual ash particles fall at a rate determined by their settling velocity in air, and deposit when they reach the ground surface.

Figure 1. Example model grids illustrated in Google Earth™[1]. (a) Latitude-longitude grid over the North Atlantic. (b) Projected grid over Alaska. (c) Close-up of cells over Redoubt volcano, showing a vertical distribution of ash specified by equation (1), using a shape factor (*k*) of 4.

---

[1]Google Earth™ images are copyrighted by Google (2011), Europa Technologies (2011), Tele Atlas, and Geocenter Consulting. Use of these and other Google Earth™ images in this document is consistent with usage allowed by Google (Google, 2013) and do not require explicit permission for publication.

Initial Conditions

Ash3d does not calculate the dynamics of a rising plume. Instead, it injects tephra into a column of cells above the volcano (fig. 1c). Users may specify that the ash be concentrated in a single cell, distributed evenly throughout the column, or distributed vertically following the Suzuki equation (fig. 1c) (Suzuki, 1983; Carey, 1996),

$$\frac{dQ_m}{dz} = Q_m \frac{k^2 (1 - z/H) \exp(k(z/H - 1))}{H[1 - (1 + k)\exp(-k)]} \, ,$$ (1)

where Q_m is the total mass of erupted material in a given time step at a given particle size, H is the total plume height, z is a given elevation in the plume, and the shape factor k is an adjustable constant that controls ash distribution with height. A low value of k gives a roughly uniform distribution of mass with elevation, while high values of k concentrate mass near the plume top.

During an eruption, Ash3d injects tephra into these cells at a constant rate. The grain-size distribution inserted into each cell in the column is the same at each elevation and for each eruptive pulse. Default values are described in section, "Web Interface."

Transport

Ash3d solves for the conservation of mass in each cell by tracking the mass concentration q with time t,

Advection-Diffusion $$\frac{\partial q}{\partial t} + \nabla \cdot ((\mathbf{u} + \mathbf{v_s})q) - \nabla \cdot (K \nabla q) = Q \, ,$$ (2)

where $\mathbf{u}$ is the 3-D wind vector, $\mathbf{v_s}$ is the settling velocity, K is the diffusivity, and Q is a source term, which is non-zero only in the column of nodes above the volcano. By default, Ash3d calculates the settling velocity of each particle size using equations of Wilson and Huang (1979) for non-spherical particles. Alternative models that can be used include an optional Cunningham slip correction factor (Seinfeld and Pandis, 2006, p. 407), which can increase the fall rate for small (<30 μm) particles at high elevation; Stokes flow; and modifications to Wilson and Huang by Ganser (1993) and Pfeiffer and others (2005).

The advection term of equation (2) (the second term on the left-hand side (LHS)) is calculated explicitly using the Donor Cell Upwind method of solution (see Schwaiger and others, 2012, for details). The diffusion term (third LHS term) is calculated implicitly at the end of each time step. The diffusivity, K, can be spatially variable and can be a function of the local meteorological conditions. We have found that our model clouds match well with observed ones when $K=0$, and have set it to this value for simulations using the web interface.

Deposition

Ash3d tracks the mass flux of each grain size across cell boundaries and accumulates a deposit once tephra falls through the cell boundary that represents the ground surface at a particular location.

Examples of Model Output

Ash3d output includes data files of the deposit (fig. 2a) and animations of the moving cloud (fig. 2b), that can be opened in Google Earth™. Other file types available are ASCII files of deposit or cloud properties that can be imported into GIS software such as ArcMap® (fig. 2c), and kml (fig. 2d) or text (fig. 2e) files illustrating the arrival time, thickness, and (optionally) grain-size distribution of tephra at airports or other locations. Ash3d also can export ASCII, binary, or NetCDF files containing the 3-D structure of the cloud at specified times. Post-processing scripts also are available that generate deposit maps and gif animations of cloud movement (cover illustration). Details are provided below.

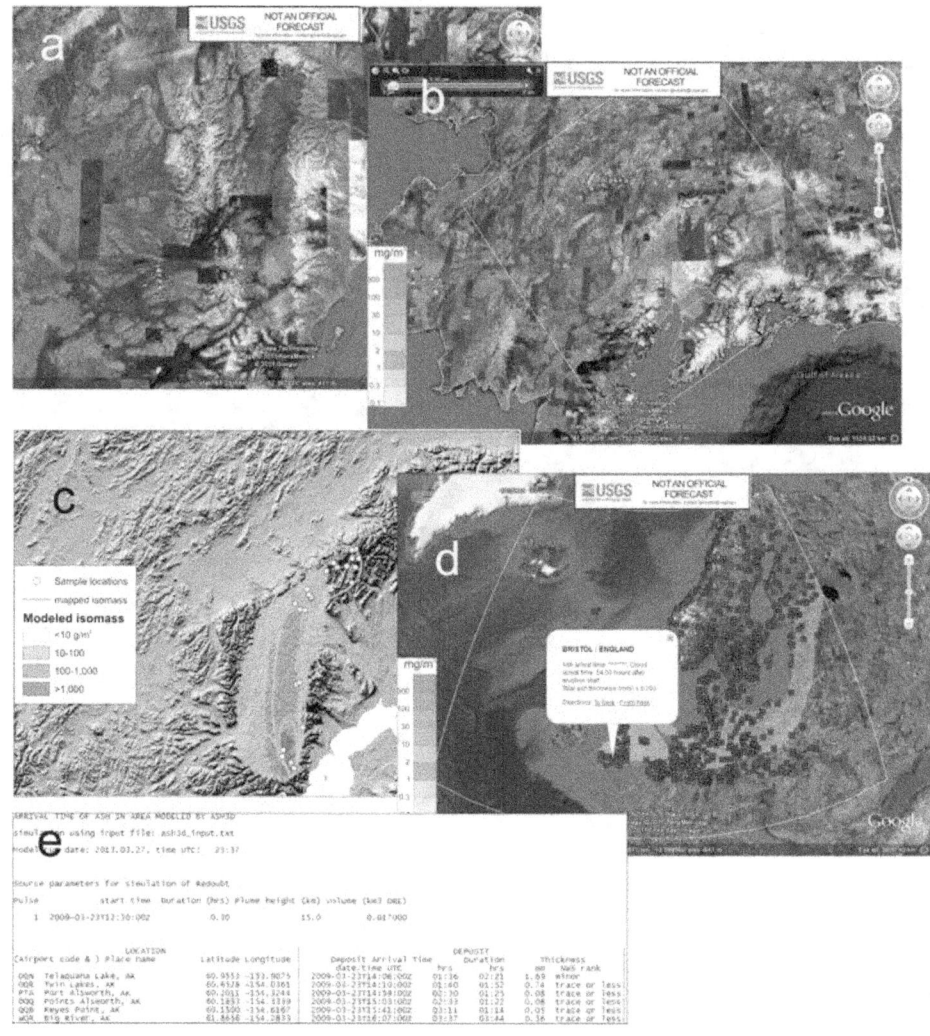

Figure 2. Examples of Ash3d output from simulations of Redoubt event 5 (Mastin and others, in press) (a, b, c, e) and Eyjafjallajökull on April 16, 2010 (Mastin and others, 2010) (d). (a) Deposit thickness illustrated in Google Earth™. (b) Cloud concentration (pink shading) in Google Earth™. (c) Deposit isomass (blue shading) in ArcMap®. (d) Cloud concentration (gray shading) and airports impacted (red squares) in Google Earth™. (e) Deposit thickness and arrival time at airports.

The Web Interface

Ash3d was written in Fortran 90/95. The program and associated scripts are executed on a Linux operating system and have been used to simulate and investigate eruptions since 2010. We strive to make it a useful operational tool, and for this purpose we designed a web interface that allows any user to quickly run the model and view results. We simplified the interface by disabling choices regarding, for example, the number of eruptive pulses, number of grain sizes, the kind of numerical weather prediction model used for the wind field, etc. that can normally be specified in Ash3d, and keeping only those few that are critical: volcano name, plume height, eruption start time, duration, erupted volume, and number of hours of simulation. We also automatically adjust model resolution so that usable results can be obtained in about 10 minutes or less.

Using the Interface

The Ash3d web interface is located at *http://vsc-ash.wr.usgs.gov*. After logging in with a username and password assigned to you, you will see a home page similar to fig. 3. Under "My Jobs", you will see a list of jobs that you have executed. Jobs that have been executed within the last 10 days will provide a link on the right-hand side to the results (under "Run Status"); older jobs are deleted automatically.

Some simulations may be shared with the public or user groups, such as the Mount St. Helens simulation shown in fig. 3. Under "Public Run Results", you may see model results that you or others have chosen to share publicly. After clicking on that link, you may also copy the URL and e-mail it to others. Anyone can see results at this URL regardless of whether they have an Ash3d account.

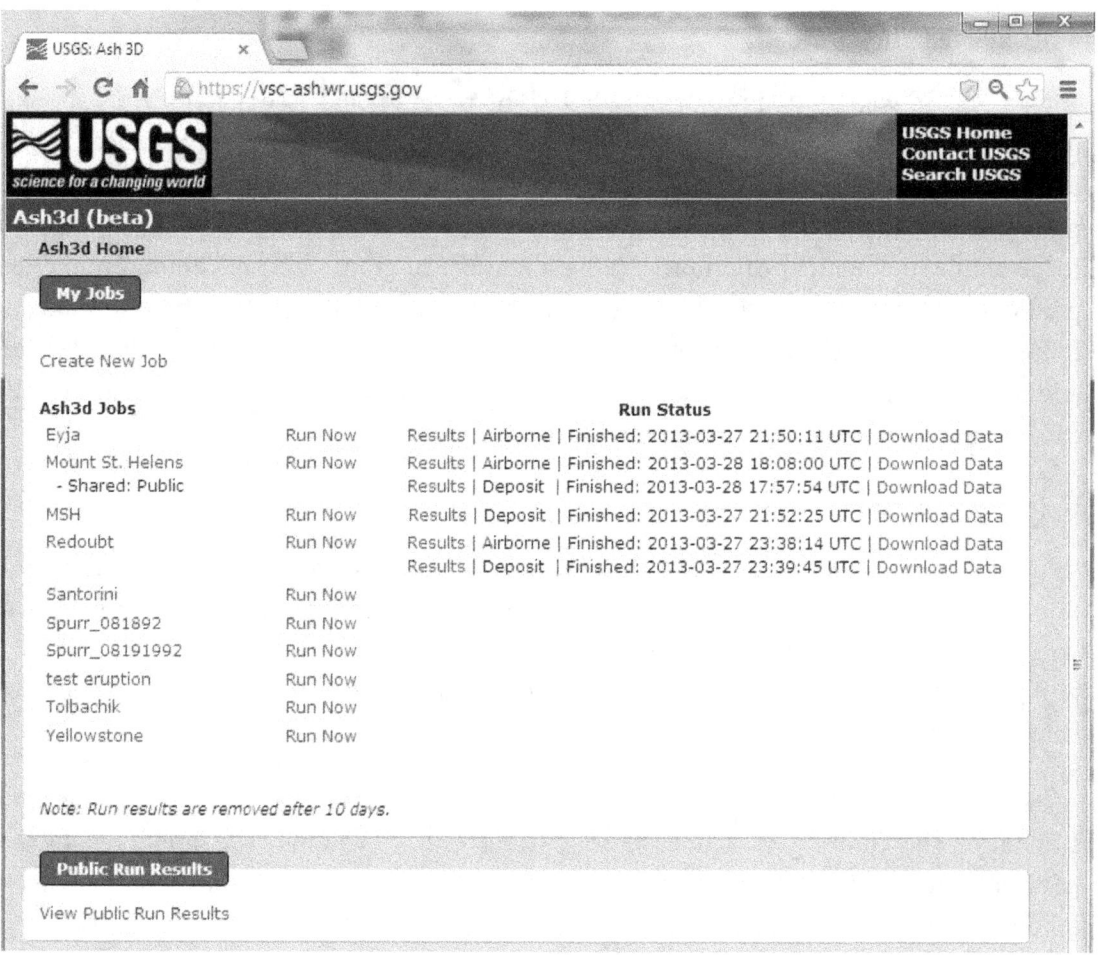

Figure 3. The Ash3d home page.

Specifying Input Values

After clicking "Create New Job" in the upper left of the home page, or clicking on any of the existing jobs, you will be sent to an Ash3d Job page that appears similar to fig. 4. This page contains the following items:

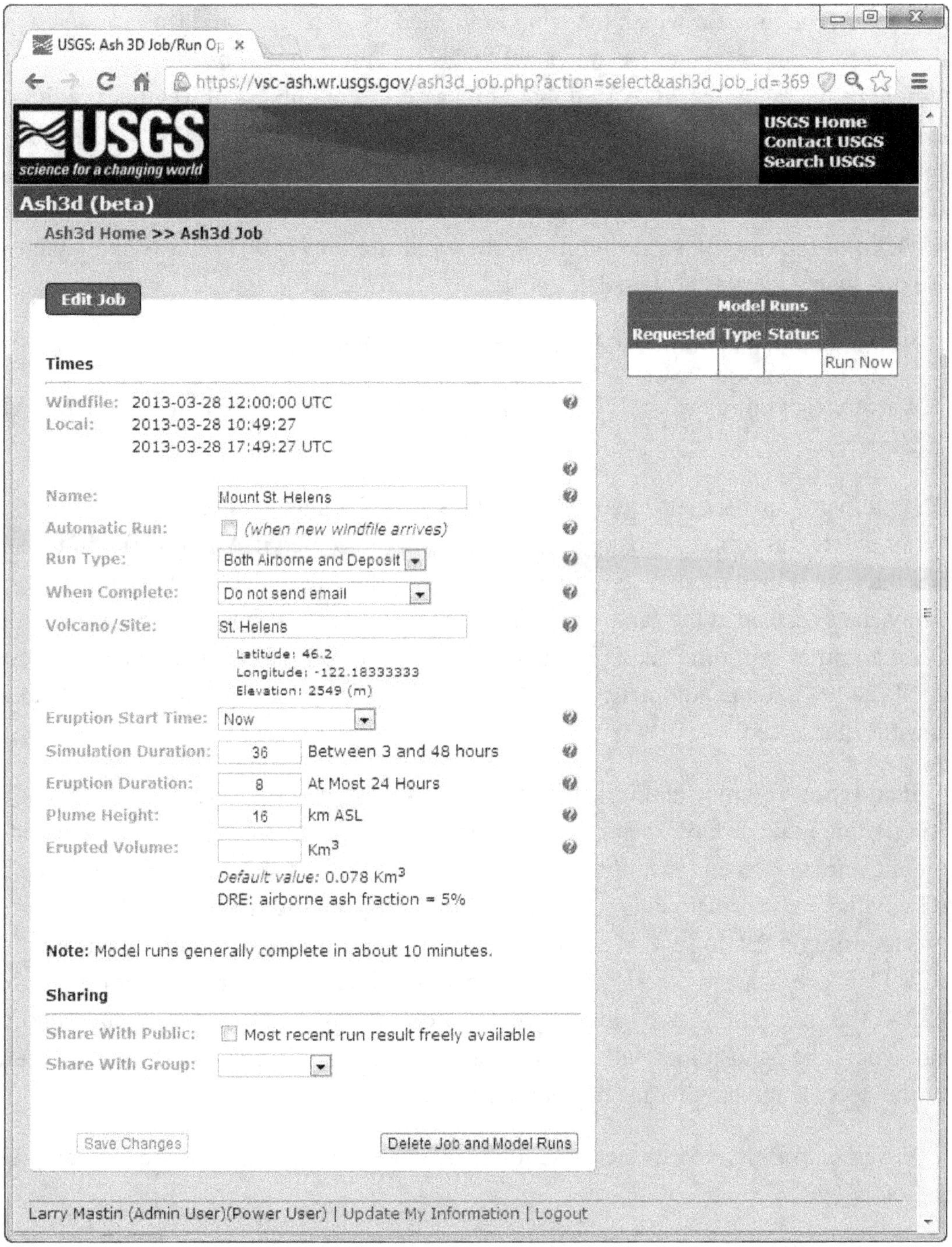

Figure 4. The Ash3d job page on the Ash3d web site.

Times: The time for which the wind field used by Ash3d is valid (top row) and the current time, in both local for your computer (second row) and UTC (third row). For forecast model runs, Ash3d uses a wind field provided by the NOAA Global Forecast System numerical weather prediction model (U.S. National Weather Service, 2013), downloaded four times daily, at 0000, 0600, 1200, and 1800 UTC. These model results typically are available on the Ash3d web interface within 5 hours after they are posted by National Oceanic and Atmospheric Administration (NOAA) (that is, at 0500, 1100, 1700, and 2300 UTC). For the case illustrated in fig. 4, the wind file for 1200 UTC was available by 1749 UTC, the time this web page was accessed.

Name: Name that you would like to apply to the current job.

Automatic run: Check this box if you would like to run this job automatically whenever a new wind file arrives.

NOTE: automatic runs are executed indefinitely, whenever a new wind file arrives, until you uncheck this box or delete this job. Automatic runs also are only executed if Ash3d is run in forecast mode, which is the case if the eruption start time is given as "now" or in "HH:MM (24 hr)". Repeat model runs will always be executed at the same time relative to the start of the wind file. For example, if you specify an eruption start time that is 6 hours after the start of the wind file, either by choosing "now" or "HH:MM (24 hr)", future automatic runs also will use an eruption start time that is 6 hours after the start of that wind file.

Run type: You may choose either airborne ash, ash deposit, or both. Airborne ash simulations use a single fine grain size (0.01 mm) with a negligible settling velocity and are intended to simulate only the movement of the cloud, not the settling of ash to form the deposit. For airborne simulations, the erupted volume in the ash cloud is set to 5 percent of the total erupted volume based on empirical studies suggesting a few to several percent of the erupted mass makes it into the distal cloud (Dacre and others, 2011; Devenish and others, 2012). Ash deposit simulations use seven grain-size bins (4, 2, 1, 0.5, 0.25, 0.125, and 0.0625 mm) and only calculate transport within several hundred kilometers of the volcano, where the deposit may fall. If "both" is specified, Ash3d runs two simultaneous simulations, one for the deposit and another for the cloud movement.

When complete: you may choose to receive an e-mail when execution is complete and results are ready to view.

Volcano/Site: start entering the name of a volcano in this text box and the interface will display the names of volcanoes from the Smithsonian Institution's *Global Volcano Program* list of active volcanoes of the world (Siebert and others, 2010) that start with these letters. You must choose one of the volcanoes whose name appears. When the latitude, longitude, and elevation labels below this text box are filled with their appropriate values, you will know that this entry was successful.

Eruption Start Time: You may choose "Now", "HH:MM (24 hr)", or "Specific Date/Time".

- "**Now**" will assign the current date and time as the eruption start time.

- "**HH:MM (24 hr)**" will assign an eruption start time by hour and minute for today or, if the time is earlier than that of the most recent wind file, for tomorrow. The time entered will be interpreted as either UTC or local time (local to your computer) depending on how your time preferences are set in the "Update My Information" link at the bottom of the page. If, for example, the current wind file is valid for today at 1200 UTC, entering an hour and minute of 0800 UTC will assign a start time of 0800 UTC TOMORROW. For the same wind file time, entering an eruption start time of 18:00 UTC would assign an eruption start time of 1800 UTC TODAY.

- "**Specific Date/Time**" allows you to enter any date from 1 January 1948 to today. If this option is chosen, the eruption is assumed to be in the past; hence, the "automatic run" checkbox, which allows future simulations to start automatically when a new wind file arrives, is automatically disabled. If you choose a date and time that is more than 2 weeks old, Ash3d will use a wind field taken from a different numerical weather prediction model; the global *NCEP/NCAR Reanalysis 1 model* with a 2.5 degree resolution (National Oceanic and Atmospheric Administration, 2013). For more recent times, Ash3d will use recently downloaded files from the NOAA Global Forecast System model.

Simulation Duration is the number of hours over which Ash3d calculates transport of the cloud. This value should be between 3 and 48 hours. Longer simulation times are not allowed because they risk exceeding the time window for which wind files are available and use wind forecasts whose reliability diminishes with time. This value is used primarily for airborne ash simulations. For deposit simulations, Ash3d calculates transport until 48 hours after the eruption starts or until 99 percent of the tephra has deposited, whichever is shorter.

Eruption duration: This is the period of active ash emission. Enter a value in hours up to 24.

Plume height: Values are given as feet or kilometers above sea level. The units are set under "Update My Information" at the bottom of this page. The NOAA/NCEP models used by Ash3d extend to a pressure level of about 1 kPa, which is roughly 34 km above sea level in the atmosphere. If you enter a plume height greater than 34 km, a warning label will appear indicating that wind vectors at elevations greater than about 34 km are assumed to be the same as the wind vectors at the highest pressure elevation.

Erupted volume is the total volume of erupted magma in cubic kilometers dense-rock equivalent (DRE). If no value is entered, the volume is automatically calculated from the plume height, eruption duration, and volcano summit elevation using the empirical relationship between plume height and eruption rate from Mastin and others (2009b, eq. 1). If the volume calculated is less than 0.001 km^3, the volume is set to 0.001 km^3 to prevent errors.

Running the Model

Once the input parameters are set and the <return> key or the "Save Changes" button in the lower left is pressed, a "Model runs" box (figs. 4 and 5) appears at the base or the right-hand side of the Ash3d job window.

Model Runs			
Requested	Type	Status	
2013-03-28 18:06:00 UTC	Airborne	Running	
2013-03-28 17:53:18 UTC	Airborne	Results	Download Data | Delete
2013-03-28 17:53:18 UTC	Deposit	Results	Download Data | Delete

Figure 5. Model Runs box, which appears in the Ash3d job page. Once changes in the input parameters are saved, a "Run Now" hyperlink is active in this list (as in the box in fig. 4). When clicked, it initiates the simulation and changes the message to "pending" or "running", as seen above. Lines below the "Running" line above give results and download links for previous simulations for this job.

Pressing the "Run Now" hyperlink in this box places this job in the queue and changes the label in the Status column to "pending," and then to "running." You can remain on this page, change to other pages in the Ash3d web interface, or log out without affecting the simulation. Once complete, the label in the Status column will change to "Results" and, as in fig. 5, other hyperlinks will appear that allow output to be downloaded or the simulation deleted. Similar links appear in the Ash3d home page (fig. 3).

NOTE: at the present time, airborne simulations typically complete in 2-3 minutes whereas deposit simulations may take 10 minutes or so due to the larger number of grain sizes whose movement must be calculated. For airborne ash, simulation times increase with plume height and simulation duration. For ash deposit runs, the time required to run the model typically increases with plume height and eruption duration.

Model Domain

As an Eulerian model, the geographic area covered by the model must be specified prior to execution. This presents a challenge; we want the domain to cover the area of the cloud or deposit, which could be east, west, north, or south of the volcano depending on wind direction; but we do not know the wind direction *a priori*. In order to set the model domain, we run a preliminary simulation at very low resolution (25×25×10 cells) over an area centered on the volcano that is large enough to completely cover the cloud or deposit. This simulation generally takes less than 1 minute to run. The calculated area of the deposit or cloud is then used to outline a smaller domain that is run at higher resolution (100×100×10 cells). This second simulation produces the final output.

Model Results Page

Upon completion, the status label in the Model Runs box changes to a hyperlink called "Results" that takes the user to a page showing model results (fig. 6). The Model Results page includes:

- A sidebar giving source parameters, the date and time of simulation and a link to download additional model output.

- A gif image (fig. 6, right) showing the distribution of the deposit or, for airborne simulations, the moving cloud.

- A list of airports impacted by ash (fig. 6, bottom). For airborne simulations, this list includes the arrival time of the cloud overhead and the number of hours during which the cloud remains overhead. For deposit simulations, the list includes the arrival time of ash on the ground and the final deposit thickness.

- A system output log, written out during model execution (out of view in fig. 6).

Clicking the "Download Data" link in the sidebar downloads a zip file containing additional maps, input files, a log file, and kmz files that can be opened in Google Earth [TM]. A list of these files is given in table 1. Detailed description of some of these files follows.

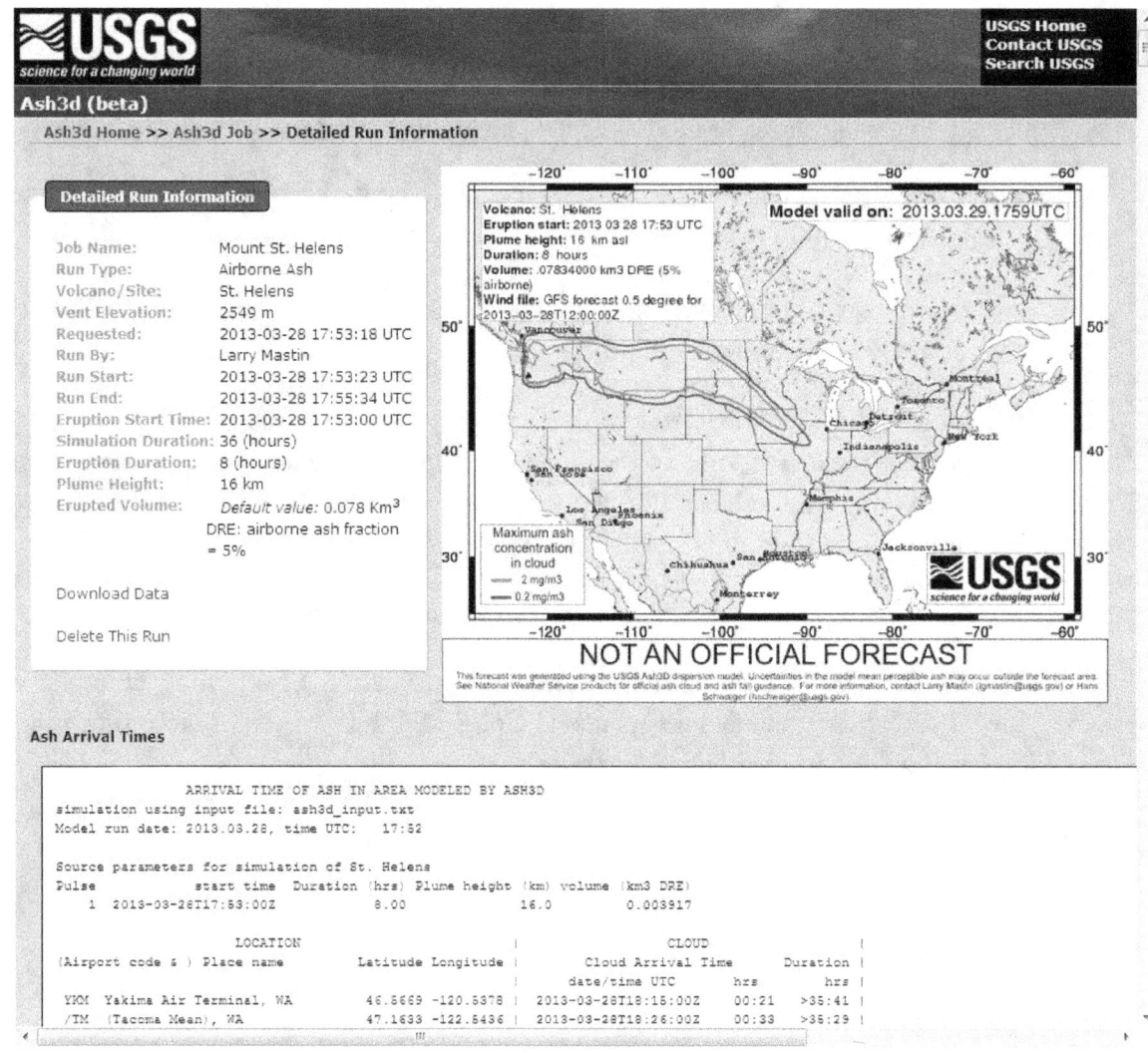

Figure 6. Results page for an airborne ash simulation at Mount St. Helens

Table 1. Files included in the zip file of model output.

[File names with an "x" in column "A" are generated during airborne simulations; those generated during deposit simulations contain an "x" in column "D"]

File name	A	D	Description
ash3d_input.txt	x	x	ASCII input file used to run this model. The contents of this file are explained below.
ashfall_arrivaltimes_airports.kmz		x	kmz file showing the locations of airports over which the ash cloud has moved or the deposit has landed.
ashfall_arrivaltimes_airports.txt		x	Text file giving the arrival time of the deposit at airports, the final deposit thickness, and the number of hours the ash will be depositing. Contents of this file are also displayed in the Results page of the web interface.
ashfall_arrivaltimes_hours.kmz		x	Static map of deposit arrival time in hours after the eruption start.
cloud_animation.gif	x		Animated map of cloud movement, with contours of concentration (0.2 and 2 mg m^{-3}), generated by combining time-stamped gif images. This animation is also displayed in the Results page of the web interface.
cloud_arrivaltimes_airports.kmz	x		kmz file showing the locations of airports over which the ash cloud has moved.
cloud_arrivaltimes_airports.txt	x		Text file giving the arrival time of the ash cloud at airports and the number of hours the cloud remains overhead. Contents of this file also are displayed in the Results page of the web interface.
cloud_arrivaltimes_hours.kmz	x		Static map of cloud arrival times in hours after the eruption start.
CloudConcentration.kmz	x		Animation of cloud movement. Colors indicate maximum ash concentration at a given x,y location.
CloudHeight.kmz	x		Animation of cloud movement. Colors indicate height of the cloud top at a given x, y location.
CloudLoad.kmz	x		Animation of cloud movement. Colors indicate integrated mass load of the cloud, in tonnes per square kilometer.
deposit_thickness_inches.gif		x	Map showing contours of deposit thickness in inches. This image is also displayed in the Results page of the web interface.
deposit_thickness_inches.kmz		x	Static map of deposit thickness in inches, with zones colored for trace, minor, substantial, etc. as given in U.S. National Weather Service (2011).
deposit_thickness_mm.gif		x	Map showing deposit thickness in contours of 0.1, 0.3, 1, 3, 10, 30, 100, and 300 mm.
deposit_thickness_mm.kmz		x	Animated map of changing deposit thickness with time and of final deposit thickness in millimeters.
NWS_Ash3d_nam242.nc	x		NetCDF output file in a format that can read by the Anchorage Volcanic Ash Advisory Center's AWIPS system.

15

File name	A	D	Description
readme.pdf	x	x	Explanation of model output along with information on how kmz files can be manipulated.
Time-stamped gif files of cloud concentration (e.g. 2012.04.11.1200UTC.gif)	x		Maps of cloud concentration, with contours of 0.2 and 2 mg m^{-3}. The time of the image is given in the file name (for example, 2012.04.11.1200UTC.gif and in the upper right-hand corner of the gif image. The time interval between these images may be 0.5, 1, 2, 3, or 6 hours depending on the length of the simulation.

Model Output Files

gif Images of the Ash Cloud or Deposit

The output from airborne ash simulations includes a series of gif files showing the location of the cloud at a given time with contours for ash concentration that coincide with current satellite detection thresholds for mass load (Prata and Prata, 2012) (0.2 mg m^{-3}, outer line) and agreed thresholds for medium to high ash concentration (International Civil Aviation Organization, 2010) (2 mg m^{-3}, inner line), (fig. 7). An animated gif image (cloud_animation.gif) is generated by combining these static images. In order to see the animation, it may be necessary to open the gif image with Microsoft Internet Explorer[TM], as many default picture viewers like Picasa[TM] will not show the animation.

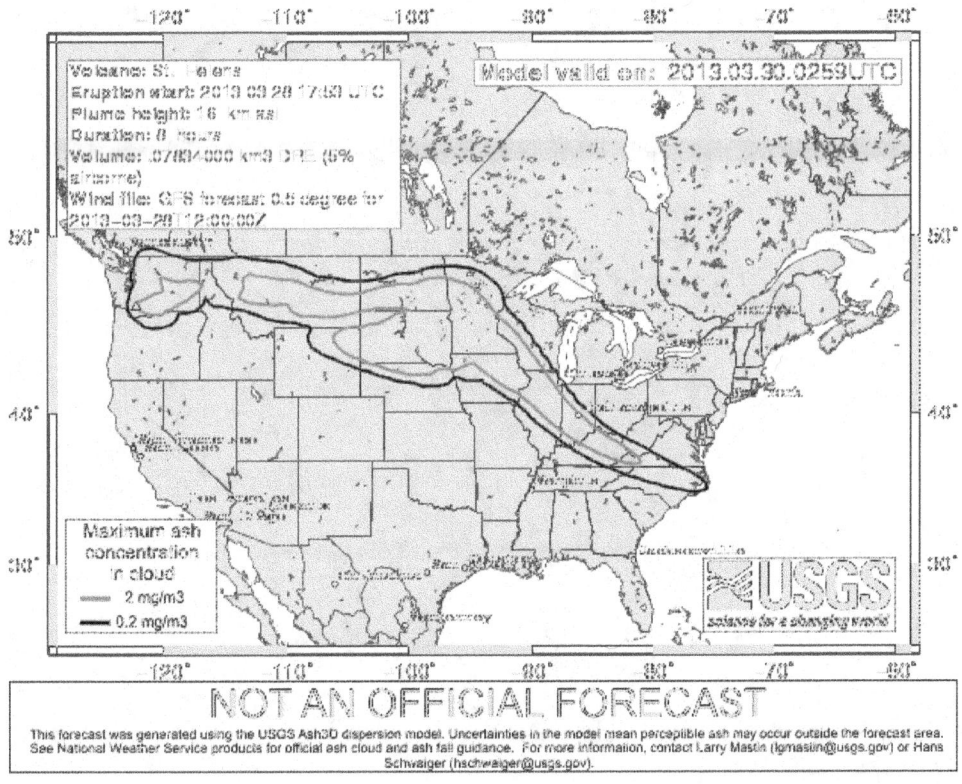

Figure 7. Gif image of an ash cloud from Mount St. Helens. The source parameters for this run are in the legend on the upper-left. The current time is given in the upper right.

17

The output from deposit simulations includes two gif images of the deposit. One (fig. 8) shows contour values of ash thickness (0.8, 6, 25, and 100 mm) that separate zones of ash impact termed "trace," "minor," "substantial," "heavy," and "severe," modified from ash impact severity terms as delineated by the USGS and the U.S. National Weather Service (U.S. National Weather Service, 2011). The second image (not shown) displays contours of 0.1, 0.3, 1, 3, 10, 30, 100, and 300 mm. Ash3d actually calculates mass load of the deposit (kg m^{-2}), and then converts this to deposit thickness assuming a deposit density of 1,000 kg m^{-3}. Measured densities of real deposits range from less than 500 (Sarna-Wojcicki and others, 1981) to greater than 1,300 kg m^{-3} (Scollo and others, 2007); hence the thickness is approximate. Using a density of 1,000 kg m^{-3}, the deposit thickness in millimeters is numerically equal to the mass load in kilograms per square meter (kg m^{-2}).

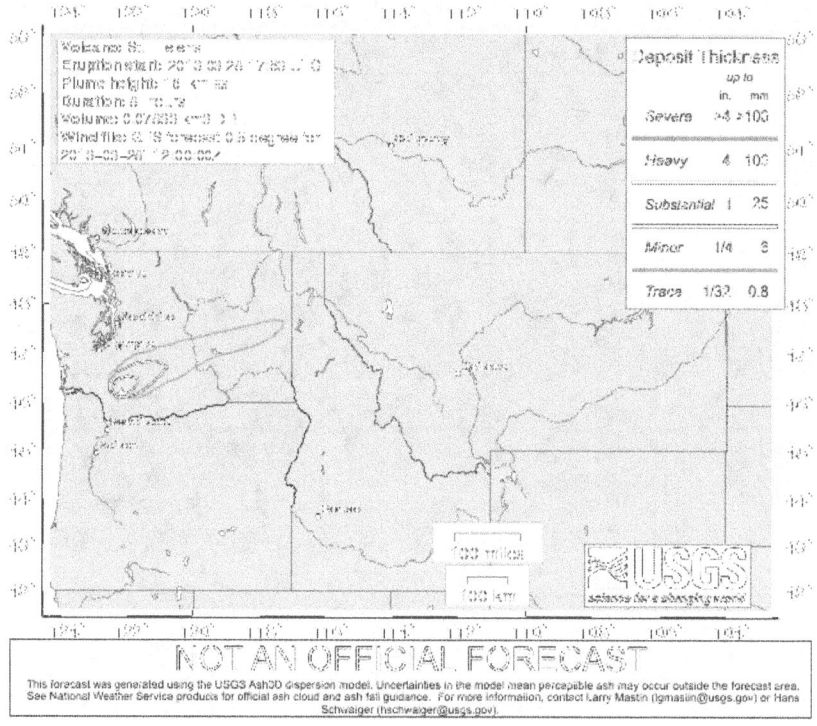

Figure 8. Gif image of the deposit distribution of a simulation from Mount St. Helens. Eruption source parameters are on the upper left.

kmz files

Files having the suffix kmz can be opened by Virtual Globes software such as Google Earth ™. These are zipped keyhole markup language (kml) files that graphically display animations of cloud movement, cloud or deposit arrival times, the thickness distribution of the deposit, and arrival times of ash at airports.

Using an example eruption from Mount St. Helens, fig. 9 illustrates the location of the cloud as displayed by the file CloudConcentration.kmz. The movement of the cloud and the appearance of impacted airports can be animated using the timeline in the upper left (label 4, fig. 9). The cloud that is visible in the Google Earth™ window is actually a set of polygons, each of which has the size and location (in 2-D) of one of the cells in the Ash3d model. When viewed from the side in Google Earth™, these polygons are located at an elevation that corresponds to the top of the cloud.

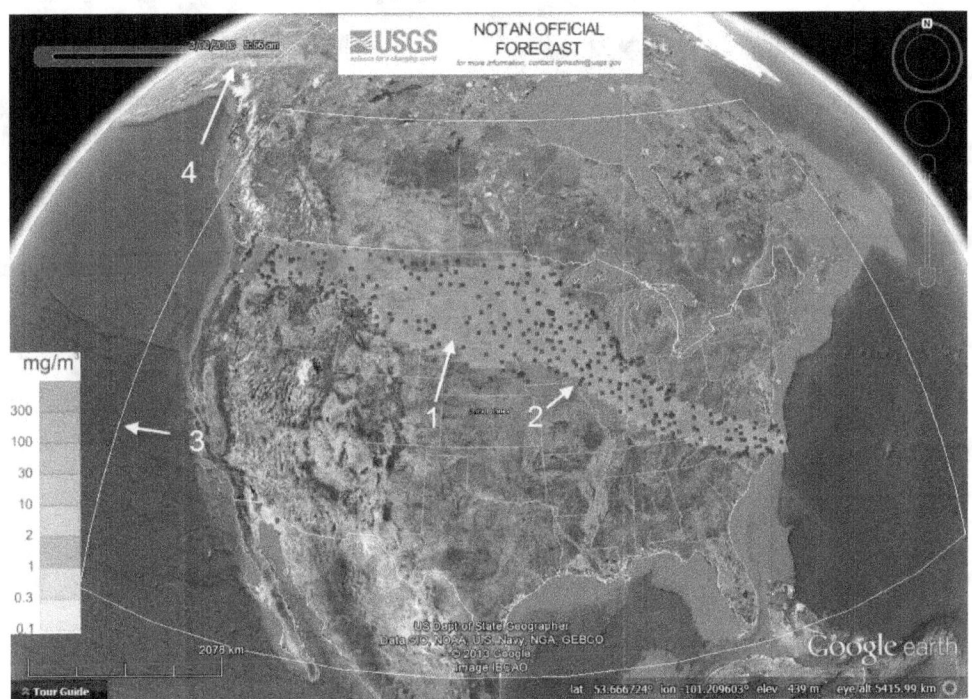

Figure 9. Google Earth ™ view of model output from a Mount St. Helens simulation from the files CloudConcentration.kmz and cloud_arrivaltimes_airports.kmz. Cloud concentration (mg m^{-3}) is shown in pink (1); impacted airports shown as red squares (2); the model boundary is shown by the white box (3). Cloud movement can be animated using the timeline (4).

To view the concentration at a particular location in the cloud, place the mouse over that location. When zoomed in, the boundaries of that node will appear (fig. 10), and the concentration value will be displayed. This display is a 2-D representation of the 3-D cloud, hence the value of ash concentration displayed is actually the maximum in a vertical column of nodes at that x and y location. Deposit thickness, cloud load and other properties are similarly displayed in other kmz files.

Figure 10. Mousing over a cloud polygon causes its outline to appear (a) and its value (here ash concentration) to be displayed.

Locations of airports (red dots) impacted by ash also are shown in fig. 9 (from the file cloud_arrivaltimes_airports.kmz). Placing the mouse arrow over any of the airport symbols causes the airport name to be displayed, and clicking on an airport symbol opens a dialog box (fig. 11). For airborne simulations, the box displays the arrival time of the cloud and the number of hours the cloud remains overhead. For deposit runs, it displays the deposit arrival time and a plot of thickness versus time at that location. In deposit simulations, which symbols denote airports where greater than 0.1 mm deposit has accumulated.

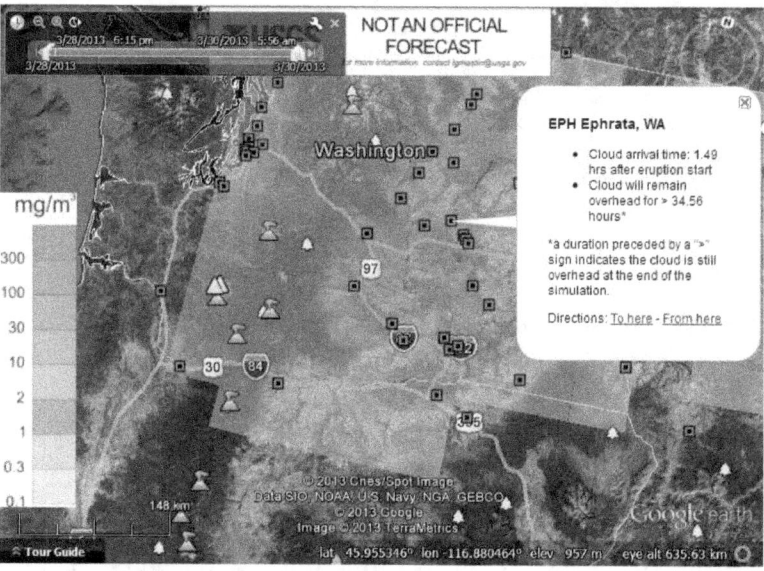

Figure 11. Clicking on an airport symbol opens a dialog box giving the arrival time of the ash cloud or deposit.

Troubleshooting kmz animations

Occasionally animations do not display properly when viewing a kmz file. Common problems and solution are:

1. *The clouds from all times are overlapping in the Google Earth* [TM] *window.* Ensure that the two caliper pincers on the timeline (b, fig. 12) are pressed together. If they are not, the timeline is set to display a time range rather than a point in time.

2. *Pressing the animation button does not make the cloud appear.* Check the timeline to make sure that the start and end times displayed correspond to the beginning and end of the simulation. If they indicate a larger time span, you may have another folder checked in "My Places" or "Temporary Places" on the left sidebar. Make sure that all other folders with time data are unchecked and try the animation again.

3. *The animation runs too slowly or too fast, or does not loop.* These settings can be adjusted by clicking on the wrench icon (c, fig. 12) on the timeline.

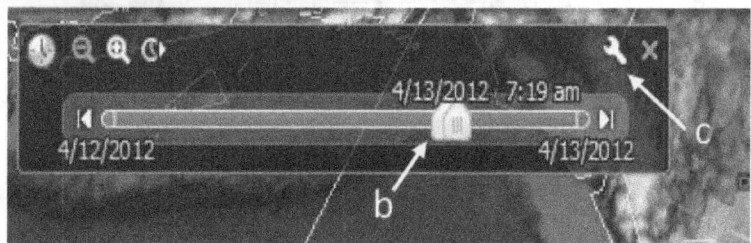

Figure 12. Close-up of the time slider in Google Earth [TM].

Manipulating the Contents of a kmz file

On the left sidebar of Google Earth [TM], under "Temporary Places," one can view the contents of the kmz file (fig. 13). The contents include a legend, a graphical USGS disclaimer, the model boundary, and a folder containing forecasts. Each subfolder in the Forecasts folder contains an image of the cloud at a time that is specified by the folder name, in year, month, day, hour, and minute (UTC). To view the cloud at just one of these specified times, uncheck the box next to the Forecasts folder, and then check a box next to a single subfolder.

Individual polygons in a subfolder also may be displayed (fig. 14) by right-clicking that subfolder, choosing "Properties," and checking the box labeled "Allow this folder to be expanded."

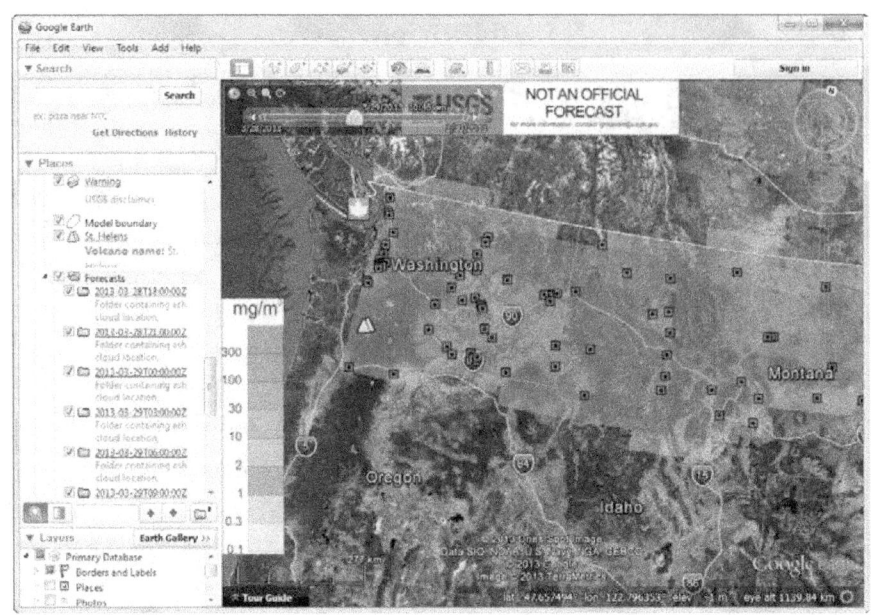

Figure 13. Google Earth ™ window with left sidebar visible, illustrating the contents of the CloudConcentration.kmz file.

Figure 14. As in fig. 13, but a subfolder has been set so that individual polygons can be viewed in the left sidebar (a).

Modeling from the Command Line

The Linux command line provides a more versatile but less user-friendly environment for running Ash3d simulations. We do not offer support for installing or running Ash3d on computers outside the USGS, but we are willing to work with collaborators who wish to run Ash3d in a more advanced environment than is possible through the web interface. Below, we explain how to set up and run a simulation in a Linux environment. Ash3d is in a state of continuing development, and we recommend that potential users consult the authors for updates before following these instructions.

Model Input Using an ASCII Input File

The Ash3d executable reads from an ASCII input file that supplies information on source parameters, output file types, and other options. A file for a simulation at Redoubt volcano is illustrated in the appendix and can be referred to from the descriptions below. All elements in blue are comments; actual input parameters are shown in black. If these files are viewed in a Linux text editor, such as vi or gedit that converts syntax elements for a shell script into colors, the same color scheme will be visible, allowing users to easily discriminate comments from parameters. The input file is further divided into blocks, delimited with lines of asterisks. Each of these blocks is described below.

Block 1: Volcano Name, Projection Parameters, Model Domain Boundaries

The lines in this block primarily define the size, shape, and location of the model domain.

Line 1 gives either the **volcano name** or the volcano's number from the Catalog of Active Volcanoes of the World (Siebert and others, 2010). If the CAVW number is given, Ash3d looks up the eruption source parameters (ESP) for this volcano in the ESP spreadsheet of Mastin and others (2009a). In the example file, the volcano name is given.

Line 2 gives the **projection parameters** for this simulation. These parameters are used to ensure that the grid coordinate system is compatible with the numerical weather prediction (NWP) model data to be used. Ash3d uses 3-D wind fields from NWP models. Once a NWP is chosen, its projection parameters must be specified. Some of those models, such as the NOAA National Center for Environmental Prediction's (NCEP) Global Forecast System (GFS) model, are run on a spherical earth, hence the wind vectors are given in a 3-D grid of latitude, longitude, and elevation. Other models, such as NOAA's North American Model use a grid that is projected onto a planar coordinate system. After Ash3d reads the NWP wind data, it must know the type of projection in order to find the portion of the NWP model grid that lies within the Ash3d model domain. Ash3d also interpolates the NWP wind field onto a new grid whose x and y axes must be parallel to that in the NWP model. For these reasons, it is necessary to know whether the NWP model uses a projected grid, and if so, the projection parameters for that grid. The types of NWP model output that Ash3d can read, and their projection parameters, are given in table 2.

Table 2. List of Numerical Weather Prediction models that Ash3d can read, and their projection parameters. The right-hand column gives the highest pressure level in the atmosphere and the approximate elevation to which this corresponds.

iwindFormat (Block 3 line 1)	NWP model type	Coordinate system used	Highest pressure level
1	1-D wind sounding	latitude/longitude must be specified in the Ash3d input, Block 1, line 2.	
2	unassigned		
3	North American Regional Reanalysis, AWIPS grid 221 (North America, 32 km resolution)[1]	Lambert Conformal Conic projection longitude of origin (λ_0)=-107° latitude of origin (ϕ_0)=50° latitude of first tangency (ϕ_1)=50° latitude of second tangency (ϕ_2)=50° Earth radius (R)=6367.47 km	**10 kPa** **(17 km)**
4	unassigned		
5	North American Model AWIPS grid 216 (Alaska, 45 km resolution)[2]	Polar Stereographic projection longitude of projection point (λ_0)=-135° latitude of projection point (ϕ_0)=90° scale factor at projection point (k_0)=0.933 Earth radius (R)=6371.229 km	**10 kPa** **(17 km)**
6	North American Model AWIPS grid 105 (polar, 90 km resolution)[3]	Polar Stereographic projection λ_0=255°, ϕ_0=90°, k_0=0.933 R=6371.229 km	
7	North American Model AWIPS grid 212 (continental U.S., 40 km resolution)[4]	Lambert Conformal Conic projection λ_0=-95°, ϕ_0=25°, ϕ_1=25°, ϕ_2=25° R=6371.229 km	**5 kPa** **(21 km)**
8	North American Model AWIPS grid 218 (continental U.S., 12 km resolution)[5]	Lambert Conformal Conic projection λ_0=-95°, ϕ_0=25°, ϕ_1=25°, ϕ_2=25°, R=6367.47 km	**5 kPa** **(21 km)**
9	unassigned		
10	North American Model AWIPS grid 242 (Alaska, 11km resolution)[6]	Polar Stereographic projection λ_0=-135°, ϕ_0=90°, k_0=0.933 R=6371.229 km	**10 kPa** **(17 km)**
11-19	unassigned		
20	NOAA Global Forecast Systsem (global, 0.5° resolution)[7]	latitude/longitude, spherical earth, radius (R) =6371.229 km	**10 kPa** **(17 km)**

iwindFormat (Block 3 line 1)	NWP model type	Coordinate system used	Highest pressure level
21	European Community Medium-Range Weather Forecasting model (ECMWF) 0.25 degree resolution	latitude/longitude, spherical earth, radius (R)=6367.47 km	**0.1 kPa** **(>50 km)**
22	NOAA Global Forecast System low-resolution (global, 2.5°)[8]	latitude/longitude, spherical earth, R=6367.47 km	**1 kPa** **(34 km)**
23	NOAA NCEP/DOE AMID II reanalysis(global, 2.5° resolution)[9]		**10 kPa** **(17 km)**
24	NASA MERRA reanalysis (global, 1.25° resolution)[10]		**0.1 kPa** **(>50 km)**
25	**NOAA NCEP Reanalysis 1 (global, 2.5° resolution)** [11]	latitude/longitude, spherical earth, R=6367.47 km	**1 kPa** **(34 km)**

[1]University Corporation for Atmospheric Research (2013a)

[2]University Corporation for Atmospheric Research (2013b)

[3]University Corporation for Atmospheric Research (2013c)

[4]University Corporation for Atmospheric Research (2013d)

[5]National Climatic Data Center (2013)

[6]University Corporation for Atmospheric Research (2013e)

[7]University Corporation for Atmospheric Research (2013f)

[8]University Corporation for Atmospheric Research (2013g)

[9]University Corporation for Atmospheric Research (2013h)

[10]National Aeronautics and Space Administration (2013)

[11]National Oceanic and Atmospheric Administration (2013)

The first two parameters on this line are `latlonflag` and `projflag`, where:

> `latlonflag` is an integer whose value is 0 if coordinate system is projected, 1 if coordinates are in latitude and longitude

> `projflag` is an integer that indicates the projection type:
> 1=Polar Stereographic
> 2=Albers Equal Area (not currently functional)
> 3=UTM (not currently functional)
> 4=Lambert Conformal Conic

Numbers that follow these are projection parameters that are different for different map projections. These parameters are explained in the comment lines above this block of input. Below are some examples of this input line. The comment in blue following the hash mark (#) gives the projection type.

```
0 1 -135.0 90.0 0.933 6371.229        #Polar stereographic
```

Parameters 3 through 6 are λ_0, the longitude of the projection point; ϕ_0, the latitude of the projection point; k_0, the scale factor at the projection point; and R, the Earth radius in kilometers.

```
0 4 -95. 25.0 25.0 25.0 6371.229  #Lambert Conformal Conic
```

Parameters 3 through 7 are λ_0, the longitude of the projection origin; ϕ_0, the latitude of the projection origin; ϕ_1, the latitude of the first secant; ϕ_2, the latitude of the second secant; and R, the Earth radius in kilometers.

Line 3 gives the x and y (or longitude and latitude) values of the **lower left corner** of the grid. These values must be in the same coordinate system defined by the projection parameters on line 2.

Line 4 gives the **model domain width and height**, in degrees if latitude and longitude are used, or kilometers if a projected coordinate system is used.

Line 5 gives the **vent location**, also in the same units as the specified coordinate system. This line may take either two or three values. The first two values are required and correspond to the x and y (or longitude and latitude) coordinates of the vent. A third, optional, value gives to the volcano's elevation in kilometers. If no elevation is given, Ash3d assigns the volcano an elevation equal to that of the topography at this location, or zero if topography is not used in this model run. For the web interface, topography is not used.

Line 6 gives the **horizontal grid spacing** in the model, in kilometers if a projected grid is used, or degrees if latitude and longitude are used. If the width and height of the model domain are not an integral number of cell distances, the location of the upper right corner of the model domain is adjusted to be an integral number of cell distances from the lower left corner.

Line 7 gives the **vertical grid spacing** of cells in the model. The units of this input parameter are always kilometers.

A note about grid spacing and model run time

    When setting up a model domain, there is a trade-off between model resolution and simulation time. Model run time is approximately proportional to the number of nodes, the number of grain sizes, and the number of time steps. On a computer with a 2.56 GHz Intel Xeon processor and 8 Gb of storage, with a Geekbench-rated floating-point performance score of 4326 (primatelabs.com, 2011), the runtime per node per time step per grain size ranges from 0.16 to 0.60 μs. Thus a simulation with a model domain of 200×200×20 nodes with 6 grain sizes and 2,500 time steps (a few tens of hours simulation time) would take about 0.5–2.0 hours to run using a single processor.

Line 8 gives the **diffusion coefficient** K and a shape factor k that determines the vertical distribution of mass in the column of nodes above the volcano. If the second parameter is a number, it is assumed to be the **Suzuki constant** k for the model run. If the second parameter is the word 'point,' all mass is placed in a single cell at the top of the plume. If the second parameter is the word 'line,' the mass is distributed evenly throughout the column of nodes above the volcano. This distribution is the same for all eruptive pulses.

Line 9 gives the **number of eruptions or eruptive pulses** in the simulation. The eruptions or eruptive pulses may be either contiguous or non-contiguous in time. Their duration should not be shorter than the average time step in the model (about a minute).

Block 2: Eruptive Pulses

The number of lines in this block equals the number of eruptions or eruptive pulses specified in line 9 of Block 1. A line of input contains three integers followed by four real numbers, for example:

```
2009 03 23 12.5   0.25  15.0   0.0018
```

The first four numbers represent the **year**, **month**, **day** and **hour** (UTC) of the start of the eruption. The following three numbers represent the **eruption duration** in hours, the **plume height** in kilometers, and the **erupted volume** (DRE) in cubic kilometers. Ash3d converts the erupted volume to a mass assuming a magma density of 2,500 kg m^{-3}.

If the year is zero as in the example input file, the model is run in forecast mode where the hour is interpreted as the number of hours after the start time of the wind file. In addition, if the duration, plume height, or erupted volume is negative, it is replaced with the default ESP value for that volcano from the spreadsheet of Mastin and others (2009a).

Block 3: Wind Files and Simulation Time

Line 1 of block 3 gives two integers, `iwind` and `iwindFormat`. `iwind` may have values 1 through 4 as described in table 3.

Table 3. List of possible values of iwind and their meanings

Value	Meaning
1	Read from 1-D wind sounding
2	Read from 3-D gridded ASCII files
3	Read directly from a single NetCDF file
4	Read directly from multiple NetCDF files

If iwind=1, Ash3d reads from an ASCII file of a 1-D wind sounding having the format shown in table 4. This option can be used if no numerical weather prediction data are available or if data from a single radiosonde measurement are deemed more reliable than NWP model results. If this option is used, then `latlonflag` (Block 2, line 1, first parameter) should be 1, indicating that no cartographic projection is used.

Table 4. Example 1-D wind sounding file in the format used by Ash3d when `iwindformat`=1. This example gives the wind sounding at Redoubt volcano during event 6 of the 2009 eruption (Wallace and others, in press). Items in blue are comments. Lines 4 and later give the elevation (m), the wind speed in m s^{-1}, and the wind direction in degrees clockwise from true north, respectively.

```
Input wind file for Ash3d
0  29                    #Wind time (hrs), number of levels of wind
-1454.327 -3482.752      #x, y Coordinates of wind profile (m)
-1      4.63   24        #elevation (m), wind speed (m/s), direction (clockwise from N)
198     4.52   24
405     4.67   25
617     4.62   24
833     6.58   33
1054    8.7    38
1281    10.4   41
1512    12.81  48
1748    12.69  53
1991    11.41  55
2241    11.01  57
2498    10.6   61
2763    9.85   70
3035    10.04  82
3315    11.79  94
3605    12.75  104
3905    12.59  112
4216    12.83  121
4541    14.51  131
4878    15.3   135
5228    14.93  134
5969    12.05  128
6778    10.99  134
7666    11.11  152
8656    10.66  152
9824    3.95   195
11294   6.77   273
13190   7.3    292
15833   9.2    290
```

When `iwind`=2, Ash3d reads a 3-D wind field in ASCII format that is converted from NetCDF format using a Java script that was originally written before Ash3d was modified to read NetCDF files directly. This option is no longer used.

`iwind`= 3 or 4 indicates that the wind files are in NetCDF format; iwind=3 for a single NetCDF file, and iwind=4 for multiple NetCDF files. The two options were created to accommodate different posting conventions for different kinds of wind files. For example, Global Forecast System output files posted at Unidata (University Corporation for Atmospheric Research, 2013e) for current and forecast conditions include a separate file for every 3-hour time step. Alaska 11 km North American Model forecasts posted at Unidata are given as a single file for multiple time steps.

The second parameter, iwindFormat, indicates the type of NWP file to be read. The values of iwindFormat for each NWP file type are listed in table 2.

Line 2 gives the integer iHeightHandler, which indicates how Ash3d should respond if it finds that the plume height exceeds the highest level in the NWP model. Numerical weather prediction models give 3-D wind fields with the vertical coordinate in pressure levels. For the GFS 0.5 degree model, the highest pressure level is ~1 kPa, which corresponds to about 34 km elevation. The wind field at higher elevation is unknown from these models. If the input plume height is higher than the highest elevation in the NWP model, Ash3d responds in one of the following ways: if iHeightHandler=1, Ash3d execution stops and writes out the following message:

```
Checking the vertical height of the mesoscale model ...
    Error: The mesoscale model grid extends to about 34. km elevation,
    but the maximum plume height extends to         50. km.
    The grid is designed to extend 30% above the maximum plume height,
    Program stopped.

    If you wish to run the simulation anyway, using
    extrapolated wind velocities at higher elevation, change the value
    of iHeightHandler to 2 in the ESP input file and rerun the model.
```

If iHeightHandler=2, Ash3d continues execution and uses the wind vectors in the top-most pressure level in all higher pressure levels. It also writes the following message to standard output and to the log file, Ash3d.lst:

```
    Checking the vertical height of the mesoscale model ...
    Warning: The highest node in the simulation domain is ~  45.0 km.
    The higest in the mesoscale file is lower, about ~  34.2 km.
    Because you have specified that
    iHeightHandler=2, all wind velocities of nodes higher than the highest
    mesoscale nodes will have wind velocities equal to that of the highest
    nearby mesoscale node.
```

Line 3 gives the simulation time in hours. The simulation time is assumed to start at the time of the first eruption or eruptive pulse. Ash3d checks the time duration of the wind files to ensure that the entire simulation time is contained within the time of the wind files.

Line 4 is a "yes" or "no" parameter that specifies whether to stop computation when 99 percent of the erupted mass has deposited. Setting this parameter to "yes" allows for faster execution if users are primarily interested in simulating deposition. If simulating ash-cloud transport is of primary interest, users may prefer to set this parameter to "no."

Line 5 specifies `nwindfiles`, the number of wind files to be read. If more than one wind file is to be read, the parameter `iwind` in Block 3, line 1, must equal 4. Ash3d assumes in that case that each wind file contains a single time slice. It examines the time stamp on the last wind file to ensure that its time is after the end time of the model simulation, and the time stamp on the first wind file to ensure that it is before the beginning of the first eruption or eruptive pulse.

Block 4: Output Options

Most lines in this block specify types of output options.

Lines 1-15 require "yes" or "no" to indicate whether a particular type of output should be written. These types of output are listed in table 5, along with the names of files written out. (Note that the file names in table 5 do not always agree with those in table 1 from the web interface).

Table 5. List of the types of output specified in the first 15 lines of block 4.

Line	Output type	File name(s)
1	ESRI® ASCII file of final deposit thickness, in millimeters	DepositFile___final.dat
2	kml file of final deposit thickness	Deposit kml
3	ESRI® ASCII files of deposit thickness (mm) at specified times	DepositFile_xxx.xhrs.dat[1]
4	kml file of deposit thickness at specified times	Deposit kml
5	ESRI® ASCII files of ash-cloud concentration at specified times. This gives the maximum concentration (in mg m^{-3}) of any cell in the column of cells at any given x, y location.	CloudConcentration_xxx xhrs.dat
6	kml file of ash-cloud concentration at specified times. This gives the maximum concentration (in mg m^{-3}) of any cell in the column of cells at any given x, y location.	CloudConcentration.kml
7	ESRI® ASCII files of ash-cloud height (km)	CloudHeight_xxx xhrs.dat
8	kml file of ash-cloud height	CloudHeight kml
9	ESRI® ASCII files of ash-cloud load (tonnes per square kilometer)	CloudLoad_xxx xhrs.dat
10	kml file of ash-cloud load	CloudLoad kml
11	ESRI® ASCII file of deposit arrival times (hours since eruption start)	DepositArrivalTime.dat
12	kml file of deposit arrival time	DepositArrivalTime.kml
13	ESRI® ASCII files of cloud arrival times (hours since eruption start)	CloudArrivalTime.dat
14	kml file of cloud arrival times	CloudArrivalTime.kml
15	3-D ash concentration at specified times	specified as input

[1]xxx.x is a number that gives the time in hours since the start of the simulation.

The **ESRI® ASCII files** noted in table 5 are ASCII files written in a format that can be directly imported into Arc® GIS products for display. They contain a six-line header followed by a 2-D matrix containing values of, for example deposit thickness, or other properties specified in table 3. The header looks like:

```
NCOLS   140
NROWS   140
XLLCORNER  -2616390.
YLLCORNER   1742330.
CELLSIZE   5000.000
NODATA_VALUE -9999.
```

The parameters XLLCORNER and YLLCORNER give the coordinates of the lower-left corner of the model domain in meters (if it is a projected grid) or degrees (if the grid is latitude/longitude). The cell size is in the same units as the corner coordinates. **Note:** the cell size printed out in these headers is the spacing in x only. Ash3d can generate grids whose x and y spacing are unequal, and this is typically the case for simulations generated using the web interface. But Arc products require the x and y spacing to be equal. **Note:** If you plan to import the ESRI® ASCII files into Arc® products, make sure to specify equal x and y cell size on line 6 of block 1.

The **kml files** are written using Keyhole Markup Language and can be opened by Google Earth [TM] or other virtual globe software. The kml files can be zipped using the following Linux command, which reduces file size by about 90–95 percent and creates a kmz file that also can be opened in Google Earth [TM]:

```
zip -r CloudLoad.kmz CloudLoad.kml
```

The **3-D ash concentration file** specified in line 15 of Table 4 contains the full 3-D distribution of each grain size in the model domain at specified times.

The following lines complete this block of input:

Line 16 specifies the **format of the 3-D ash concentration file.** Options are 'ascii,' 'binary,' or 'netcdf.' NetCDF is a standard format for atmospheric model data and is most frequently used by us.

Line 17 gives nWriteTimes, the number of times data are to be written out to the files above. Data may be written out at uneven intervals (for example, 0.2, 3, 3.4, and 12 hours after the eruption start) or at even intervals (for example, every 2 hours, starting 2 hours after the eruption start).

Line 18 gives the times at which output is written:

If nWriteTimes>0, line 18 should contain nWriteTimes numbers, in increasing order, which specify the times in hours after the start of the eruption at which the above data are to be written.

If nWriteTimes=-1, line 18 should contain a single number indicating the time interval in hours between write times.

Block 5: Input Wind files

This block should contain a number of lines equal to nWindFiles (block 3, line 5). Unless iwindFormat (block 3, line 1) is 1 or 2, these files should be in NetCDF format and should consist of output from one of the model types listed in table 1. Each line gives the file name and path. In the example file, Ash3d reads a single wind file named latest.nc, located in the subdirectory Wind_nc. Ash3d opens this file and does a preliminary read to ensure that it covers the time period and geographic region specified in input.

Downloading and Converting Wind Files for Use by Ash3d

The NetCDF files used by Ash3d are available at several repositories which are listed in footnotes to table 2. Here we give an example illustrating how we download and convert two of these files, the NOAA National Center for Environmental Prediction (NCEP) North American Model for Alaska, run on an 11 km nodal resolution; and the NASA MERRA global 1.25° reanalysis. The first of these examples is the NWP model specified as input in the example input file.

1) We use a shell script with the following wget command,

```
            wget \
http://motherlode.ucar.edu:8080/thredds/fileServer/fmrc/NCEP/NAM/Alaska_11km/files/NAM_Alaska_11km_20110909_0000.grib2,
```

which retrieves the output file for September 9, 2011, 00Z from the motherload repository at the University Corporation of Atmospheric Research (UCAR). (This repository only holds current model output, so this particular date may be unavailable at the time you read this).

The data are compressed in grib2 format. We convert them to NetCDF format using the NetCDF-java package distributed through Unidata (University Corporation for Atmospheric Research, 2013i). This package is distributed as a single .jar (Java archive) file, `netcdfAll-4.1.jar`, which we place in the directory `~/ncj`. We then run the following command:

```
java -Xmx2048m -classpath ~/ncj/netcdfAll-4.1.jar ucar.nc2.dataset.NetcdfDataset \

            -in NAM_Alaska_11km_20110909_0000.grib2 -out latest.nc -IsLargeFile
```

This command takes the grib2 file `NAM_Alaska_11km_20110909_0000.grib2` and converts it into the NetCDF file, `latest.nc`, which is used as input to the Ash3d model. In order for Ash3d to properly read this file, we must set `iwindFormat` to 10 (block 3, line 1). Model nodes in these files are set up on a grid of 11 km latitude and longitude on a polar stereographic projection. Therefore we must also set `latlonflag` to 0 and `projflag` to 2 (block 1, line 2), and use the projection parameters given in the example input file.

Note: if reading from NCEP/NCAR global reanalysis files (iwindFormat=25), then `nWindFiles` should equal 1 and block 5 should contain a single line giving the path to the directory that contains the NCEP/NCAR global reanalysis files. Subdirectories within this directory should be named by year (for example, "2012").

Block 6: Arrival Times at Airports

The input lines in this block specify whether arrival times and other information at specific locations are to be written to output. Normally, Ash3d reads from a text input file containing the latitude and longitude (or x and y locations) of a list of points. For the web interface, this is a global list of airports, but when hand-editing the ASCII input file, other lists, such as sample locations, also may be specified. Ash3d can then generate either text or kml files listing the subset of these locations where ash was deposited or where the cloud passed overhead. Ash3d also can write out the grain-size distribution of points at those locations. All but line 4 require "yes" or "no" parameters.

Line 1 indicates whether to write out ash arrival times at these locations to an ASCII file. If "yes" is given, an output file is generated called `AshArrivalTimes.txt` with output in the format shown in fig. 2e.

Line 2 indicates whether the ASCII output file should give a grain-size distribution of the tephra deposit at each location.

Line 3 indicates whether to write out a kml file showing the locations that will be impacted by ash. If "yes" is given, a file named `AshArrivalTimes.kml` is generated that plots each impacted location as a red placemarks as shown in fig. 2d.

Line 4 gives the name and path of the file containing airports or other locations of interest.

Line 5 indicates whether Ash3d should use the projection utility to calculate projected coordinate locations. This parameter should be set to "yes" if a projected coordinate system is used. If set to "yes", projections are performed using the projection parameters given in block 1, line 2.

Block 7: Grain-Size Groups

Ash3d can run an unlimited number of grain sizes, although the required run time increases roughly in proportion to the number of grain sizes. To reduce model run time, Ash3d stops calculations for individual grain sizes once they have deposited. When simulating ash clouds, one very small grain size (0.01 mm for example) with a very low settling velocity is frequently adequate to display general cloud movement. When simulating deposits, it is best to use at least a half dozen grain sizes: fewer grain sizes tend to produce secondary thickness maxima as an artifact (Mastin and others, in press).

Line 1 of block 7 consists first of an integer giving the number of size bins (`nsize`). Optionally, a second integer can be provided which specifies the fall model to be used (`FV_ID`). If `FV_ID` is not given or `FV_ID=1`, the Wilson and Huang (1979) model is used. If `FV_ID=2`, the Wilson and Huang model with a slip-flow correction is used (Seinfeld and Pandis, 2006). If `FV_ID=3`, the modification to the Wilson and Huang model outlined by Pfeiffer and others (2005) is used. If `FV_ID=4`, the model of Ganser (1993) is used. If `FV_ID=5`, Stokes flow for spherical particles with a slip-flow correction is used.

Subsequent lines. The first line is followed by `nsize` lines, one for each bin size. These lines may contains two, three, or four numerical parameters:

- If two parameters, Ash3d reads the first as the mass fraction of that size bin, and the second as the settling velocity in m s^{-1}. Ash3d uses this as a constant settling velocity, independent of elevation.

- If three parameters, Ash3d reads the first as grain size in millimeters, the second as the mass fraction, and the third as the density in kg m^{-3}. Ash3d calculates settling velocity of these particles assuming a shape factor (*f*) of 0.44, which is the average of values measured by Wilson and Huang (1979). The settling velocity in this case depends on air density and viscosity. Air density is calculated from the pressure and temperature at a given elevation (obtained from the NWP model data). The viscosity is calculated from Sutherland's Law (Jacobson, 2005, p. 201).

- If four parameters, Ash3d reads the first three as before, and the last as the shape factor f, defined as $f=(b+c)/2a$, where a, b, and c are the semimajor, intermediate, and semiminor axes of an ellipsoid.

Block 8: Locations of Vertical Profiles

In some cases, it has been useful to plot vertical profiles through the ash cloud, as for example, when ground-based LiDAR data were available over Europe during the 2010 eruption of Eyjafjallajökull. In that case, the lines in block 8 appeared as follows:

```
4                         #number of locations for vertical profiles (nlocs)
12.4   51.4               #Leipzig
11.3   48.2               #Munich (Maisach)
11.0   47.4               #Schneefernerhaus (Zugspitze)
11.0   47.8               #Hohenpeissenberg
```

The first line contains an integer indicating the number of locations (nlocs) where vertical profiles are to be recorded. If nlocs=0 (as in the example input file), no lines follow in this block. Otherwise, nlocs lines follow, giving the locations for each profile in the coordinate system appropriate for this model run (in this case, degrees longitude and latitude, respectively). The blue comment lines give the names of these locations.

Upon execution, Ash3d writes out text files with the names vprofile01.txt, vprofile02.txt, vprofile03.txt, vprofile04.txt, containing vertical profiles at each of these locations. Below is a truncated illustration of the output contained in vprofile01.txt:

```
Vertical profile data for location
x:     12.400
y:     51.400
                              Output is ash concentration in mg/m3
                              elevation (km) ---->
date-time          hrs            0.250          0.750           1.250
2010041601.12,     40.120,    0.000E+00,     -0.106E-65,     0.931E-62, . . .
2010041601.34,     40.345,    0.000E+00,     -0.927E-62,     0.288E-58, . . .
2010041601.57,     40.570,    0.000E+00,     -0.655E-58,     0.336E-54, . . .
2010041601.80,     40.796,    0.000E+00,     -0.201E-53,     0.234E-49, . . .
2010041602.02,     41.024,    0.000E+00,     -0.323E-49,     0.678E-46, . . .
2010041602.25,     41.251,    0.000E+00,     -0.419E-47,     0.509E-44, . . .
2010041602.48,     41.479,    0.000E+00,     -0.934E-45,     0.246E-41, . . .
.
```

The header gives the x and y coordinates of this location. The numbers in the first row of the table, "0.250", "0.750", "1.250", etc., are the elevations (km) of each cell center in the model. Each row of data following contains the date and time (UTC, in yyyymmddhh.hh), the number of hours after the beginning of the eruption, and the concentrations (mg m^{-3}) of tephra at each elevation. Ash3d writes out a line of output every 10 time steps as long as the cloud is passing overhead.

Block 9: Comment Lines and Topography

Line 1 of this block gives the name of the output file containing the 3-D cloud structure, if this output is specified in line 15 of block 4.

Line 2 gives the title of the simulation. If the 3-D cloud structure is written out to a NetCDF file (as specified in line 16 of block 4), this title is included in that file.

Line 3 gives an optional comment that may be written out to the same NetCDF file.

Line 4 allows users to specify whether topography is used in this model simulation. Ash3d uses either of two world topography databases, the GEBCO_08 Global Topography (British Oceanographic Data Centre, 2013) and ETOPO1 (Amante and Eakins, 2009). The GEBCO_08 database gives both topography and bathymetry of the ocean basins, though Ash3d assigns zero elevation to all points whose elevation lies below sea level (locations like Death Valley, where elevation is below sea level are deemed infrequent enough not to present a major problem). The GEBCO_08 database has a 30 arc-second resolution (<900 m), while the ETOPO01 database has a 1 arc-minute resolution. Both have a finer resolution than all NWP models.

Line 5 specifies the topography file format and the smoothing length of topography. The first parameter is an integer whose value is 1 if ETOPO1 topography is used, and 2 if GEBCO_08 topography is used. The second parameter is a real number indicating the smoothing length (in km) of the topography. The topography is smoothed over a particular region in order to minimize spurious or isolated patches of deposit that develop as a model artifact due to topography. Topography is smoothed using a cubic spline interpolant.

Line 6 gives the name of the topography file used. These files are in NetCDF format.

Running Ash3d

Ash3d and its associated scripts have been written on a Linux operating system. We have installed it to date on several Linux computers running Ubuntu[TM] Fedora[TM], and CentOS[TM]. Before running Ash3d, make sure that the directory containing the executable program (Ash3d) is in your PATH setting, and type:

```
Ash3d input_filename
```

After being launched, Ash3d checks the input data for errors and writes the input parameters to standard output and to the log file Ash3d.lst. Ash3d then begins the simulation, writing a table of output containing the following information.

```
Starting volume (km3 DRE)    =      0.0000
maximum number of time steps =      2475
```

	Time		|------------Volume (km3 DRE)------------|			Cloud Area
step	(hrs)	yyyymmddhh:mm	Deposit	Aloft	Outflow	Total	km2
10*	0.036	2011091613:02	0.00000	0.00029	0.00000	0.00029	2400.0
20	0.077	2011091613:04	0.00001	0.00058	0.00000	0.00058	3200.0
30	0.117	2011091613:07	0.00001	0.00086	0.00000	0.00087	3200.0
40	0.158	2011091613:09	0.00002	0.00114	0.00000	0.00117	4000.0
50	0.198	2011091613:11	0.00004	0.00142	0.00000	0.00146	4800.0

```
60      0.239   2011091613:14   0.00006   0.00169   0.00000   0.00175   5200.0
70      0.279   2011091613:16   0.00009   0.00171   0.00000   0.00180   5600.0
.
.
.
```

This output continues until either the time equals the specified simulation time, or 99 percent of the tephra mass has been deposited, depending on the stated input conditions (block 3, line 3). At the end the simulation time (10 hours in this case), Ash3d writes out statistics that include the execution time, the simulation time, the total volume accounted for in the model, the maximum deposit thickness and statistics on cloud load:

```
.
.
.
820     8.677   2011091621:40   0.00170   0.00009   0.00000   0.00179   108800.0
830     9.016   2011091622:00   0.00171   0.00008   0.00000   0.00178   109200.0
840     9.355   2011091622:21   0.00172   0.00006   0.00000   0.00178   108800.0
850     9.695   2011091622:41   0.00172   0.00006   0.00000   0.00178   109600.0
860*   10.000   2011091623:00   0.00173   0.00005   0.00000   0.00178   113600.0
*=files written out

Number of airports impacted by ash =  36

    Execution time           =        61.3900 seconds
    Simulation time          =     36121.7520 seconds
    Execution time/CPU time  =       588.3980
    Ending deposit volume    =         0.0017 km3 DRE
    Ending total volume      =         0.0018 km3 DRE

    Maximum deposit thickness (mm)  =      1.7039
    Area covered by >0.01 mm (km2)  =     42000.0


    Writing out ESRI ASCII deposit file

    Closing kml cloud concentration file

    Closing kml cloud height file

    Closing kml cloud load file

    Closing kml deposit file
    Writing kml deposit arrival time file

    Writing ASCII deposit arrival time file

    Writing to kml cloud arrival time file

    Writing to ASCII cloud arrival time file


Ash load    cloud area
   T/km2          km2
     0.2     113600.0
     1.0      59600.0
     2.0       8800.0
     4.0          0.0
     6.0          0.0
```

Ash3d also can be run interactively with no command-line arguments given. In this case, the user will be prompted for the name of the input file. After entering the input file name, Ash3d will ask if it should load a concentration file. If 'no', the simulation proceeds as if the input file was given on the command-line. If 'yes', then the name of a netCDF output file from a prior Ash3d run is requested. The user is then prompted for the time step to be used for initializing the concentration. This output netCDF file must be compatible with the parameters in the input file. This feature provides a way for lengthy simulations to be restarted if there was an error in an earlier run (power failure, IO error, etc.)

Getting Help at the Command Line

Online help for running Ash3d can be obtained by typing the following at the command line:

```
Ash3d -h      or    Ash3d -h run
            : gives information on how to execute    call help_run()

Ash3d -h input
            : gives information on input file format    call help_input(0)

Ash3d -h make
            : gives information on the different make options    call help_make()

Ash3d -h wind
            : gives information on the different wind
            files, where to get them, etc.
 call help_wind()
```

Concluding Remarks

Ash3d is in a continual state of development. The current document explains the capabilities of the model in its current form, version 526 in the vsc-ash branch of our svn repository. However we expect significant changes in future years. This document may be superseded by later versions.

References Cited

Amante, C., Eakins, B.W., 2009, ETOPO1 1 Arc-Minute Global Relief Model: Procedures, Data Sources, and Analysis, NOAA Technical Memorandum NESDIS NGDC-24, National Oceanic and Atmospheric Administration National Geophysical Data Center, Boulder, CO, 19pp, (data available at *http://www.ngdc.noaa.gov/mgg/global/global.html*).

British Oceanographic Data Centre, 2013, General Bathymetric Chart of the Oceans, accessed March 27, 2013, at *https://www.bodc.ac.uk/data/online_delivery/gebco/gebco_08_grid/*

Carey, S., 1996, Modeling of tephra fallout from atmospheric eruptions, *in* Scarpa, L.A., and Tilling, R.I., eds., Monitoring and Mitigation of Volcanic Hazards: Berlin, Springer Verlag, p. 429-463.

Dacre, H.F., Grant, A.L.M., Hogan, R.J., Belcher, S.E., Thomson, D.J., Devenish, B., Marenco, F., Haywood, J., Ansmann, A., and Mattis, I., 2011, The structure and magnitude of the ash plume during the initial phase of the Eyjafjallajökull eruption, evaluated using lidar observations and NAME simulations: Journal of Geophysical Research, v. 116, D00U03,doi 10.1029/2011JD015608.

Devenish, B., Francis, P.N., Johnson, B.T., Sparks, R.S.J., and Thomson, D.J., 2012, Sensitivity analysis of dispersion modeling of volcanic ash from Eyjafjallajökull in May 2010: Journal of Geophysical Research, v. 117, (D00U21), doi:10.1029/2011JD016782.

Ganser, G.H., 1993, A rational approach to drag prediction of spherical and nonspherical particles: Powder Technology, v. 77, p. 143-152.

Google, 2013, Permission Guidelines for Google Maps and Google Earth: accessed March 27, 2013 at *http://www.google.com/permissions/geoguidelines.html*.

Harris, A.J.L., Gurioli, L., Hughes, E.E., and Lagreulet, S., 2012, Impact of the Eyjafjallajökull ash cloud: A newspaper perspective: Journal Geophysical Research, v. 117, B00C08, doi 10.1029/2011jb008735.

International Civil Aviation Organization, 2010, Volcanic Ash Contingency Plan: EUR and NAT Regions, EUR Doc 019, NAT Doc 006, Part II, 26 p.: International Civil Aviation Organization, Montreal, Canada.

Jacobson, M.Z., 2005, Fundamentals of Atmospheric Modeling: Cambridge, Cambridge University Press, 813 p.

Mastin, L.G., Schwaiger, H., and Denlinger, R., 2010, Why do models predict such large ash clouds? An investigation using data from the Eyjafjallajökull eruption, Iceland: EOS, Transactions of American Physical Union, Fall Meeting, Abstract V54C-03.

Mastin, L.G., Guffanti, M., Ewert, J.W., and Spiegel, J., 2009a, Spreadsheet of eruption source parameters for active volcanoes of the world: U.S. Geological Survey Open-File Report 2009-1133, 6 p.

Mastin, L.G., Schwaiger, H., Schneider, D.J., Wallace, K.L., Schaefer, J., and Denlinger, R.P., in press, Injection, transport, and deposition of tephra during event 5 at Redoubt Volcano, March 23, 2009: Journal of Volcanology and Geothermal Research, doi 10.1016/j.jvolgeores.2012.04.025.

Mastin, L.G., Guffanti, M., Servranckx, R., Webley, P., Barsotti, S., Kean, K., Durant, A., Ewert, J.W., Neri, A., Rose, W.I., Schneider, D., Siebert, L., Stunder, B., Swanson, G., Tupper, A., Volentik, A., and Waythomas, C.F., 2009b, A multidisciplinary effort to assign realistic source parameters to models of volcanic ash-cloud transport and dispersion during eruptions: Journal of Volcanology and Geothermal Research, v. 186, p. 10-21.

National Aeronautics and Space Administration, 2013, Global Modeling and Assimilation Office, MERRA: Modern-Era Retrospective Analysis for Research and Applications: accessed March 27, 2013 at *http://gmao.gsfc.nasa.gov/merra/*.

National Climatic Data Center, 2013, NOAA National Operational Model Archive & Distribution System: NOMADS Data Access: accessed March 27, 2013 at *http://nomads.ncdc.noaa.gov/data.php?name=access#hires_weather_datasets*.

National Oceanic and Atmospheric Administration, 2013, Earth System Research Laboratory NCEP/NCAR Reanalysis 1: accessed March 27, 2013 at *http://www.esrl.noaa.gov/psd/data/gridded/data.nmc.reanalysis.html*

Pfeiffer, T., Costa, A., and Macedonio, G., 2005, A model for the numerical simulation of tephra fall deposits: Journal of Volcanology and Geothermal Research, v. 140, no. 3, p. 273-294.

Prata, A.J., and Prata, A.T., 2012, Eyjafjallajökull volcanic ash concentrations determined using Spin Enhanced Visible and Infrared Imager measurements: Journal of Geophysical Research, v. 117, D00U23,doi 10.1029/2011jd016800.

primatelabs.com, 2013, Linux PC (Intel® Xeon® CPU *L5520@2.27GHz*), Accessed March 26, 2013, at *http://browser.primatelabs.com/geekbench2/242143*, 1p.

Sarna-Wojcicki, A.M., Shipley, S., Waitt, R., Dzurisin, D., and Wood, S.H., 1981, Areal distribution, thickness, mass, volume, and grain size of air-fall ash from the six major eruptions of 1980, *in* Lipman, P.W., and Christiansen, R.L., The 1980 Eruptions of Mount St. Helens, Washington: U.S. Geological Survey Professional Paper 1250, p. 577-601.

Schwaiger, H., Denlinger, R., and Mastin, L.G., 2012, Ash3d: a finite-volume, conservative numerical model for ash transport and tephra deposition: Journal of Geophysical Research, v. 117, B04204,doi 10.1029/2011JB008968.

Scollo, S., Del Carlo, P., and Coltelli, M., 2007, Tephra fallout of 2001 Etna flank eruption—Analysis of the deposit and plume dispersion: Journal of Volcanology and Geothermal Research, v. 160, p. 147-164.

Seinfeld, J.H., and Pandis, S.N., 2006, Atmospheric Chemistry and Physics: From Air Pollution to Climate Change: Hoboken, New Jersey, John Wiley & Sons, 1,203 p.

Siebert, L., Simkin, T., and Kimberly, P., 2010, Volcanoes of the World, Third ed.: Washington D.C., Smithsonian Institution, 551 p. Data accessed March, 2009 from *http://www.volcano.si.edu*.

Suzuki, T., 1983, A theoretical model for dispersion of tephra, *in* Shimozuru, D., and Yokoyama, I., Arc Volcanism—Physics and Tectonics: Tokyo, Terra Scientific Publishing Company, p. 95-113.

U.S. National Weather Service, 2011, Volcanic ashfall event—Product and statement guidance for Alaska Region: accessed March 15, 2013, at *http://www.arh.noaa.gov/essd/docs/Volcanic%20Ashfall%20Event_product%20and%20statement%20guidelines.pdf*, 1 p.

U.S. National Weather Service, 2013, Environmental Modeling Center, Global Forecast System: accessed March 27, 2013, at *http://www.emc.ncep.noaa.gov/index.php?branch=GFS*.

University Corporation for Atmospheric Research, 2013a, CISL Research Data Archive: NCEP North American Regional Reanalysis: accessed March 27, 2013 at *http://rda.ucar.edu/datasets/ds608.0/*

University Corporation for Atmospheric Research, 2013b, Dataset: NCEP Model Data/North American Model (NAM)/NCEP-NAM-Alaska_45km: accessed March 27, 2013 at *http://motherlode.ucar.edu:8080/thredds/idd/models.html?dataset=FMRC/NCEP/NAM/Alaska_45km*.

University Corporation for Atmospheric Research, 2013c, Dataset: NCEP-NAM-Polar_90km: accessed March 27, 2013 at *http://motherlode.ucar.edu:8080/thredds/catalog/fmrc/NCEP/NAM/Polar_90km/catalog.html*.

University Corporation for Atmospheric Research, 2013d, Dataset: NCEP-NAM-CONUS_40km-conduit: accessed March 27, 2013 at *http://motherlode.ucar.edu:8080/thredds/catalog/fmrc/NCEP/NAM/CONUS_40km/conduit/catalog.html*.

University Corporation for Atmospheric Reseaerch, 2013e, Dataset: NCEP-NAM-Alaska_11km: accessed March 27, 2013 at *http://motherlode.ucar.edu:8080/thredds/catalog/fmrc/NCEP/NAM/Alaska_11km/catalog.html*.

University Corporation for Atmospheric Research, 2013f, Dataset: NCEP-GFS-Global_0p5deg: accessed March 27, 2013 at *http://motherlode.ucar.edu:8080/thredds/catalog/fmrc/NCEP/GFS/Global_0p5deg/catalog.html*

University Corporation for Atmospheric Research, 2013g, Dataset: NCEP-GFS-Global_2p5deg: accessed March 27, 2013 at *http://motherlode.ucar.edu:8080/thredds/catalog/fmrc/NCEP/GFS/Global_2p5deg/catalog.html*.

University Corporation for Atmospheric Research, 2013h, CISL Research Data Archive: NCEP/DOE Reanalysis II: accessed March 27, 2013 at *http://rda.ucar.edu/datasets/ds091.0/*.

University Corporation for Atmospheric Research, 2013i, Netcdf-Java: accessed March 27, 2013 at *http://www.unidata.ucar.edu/software/netcdf-java/*.

Wallace, K.L., Schaefer, J., and Coombs, M.L., in press, Character, mass, distribution, and origin of tephra-fall deposits from the 2009 eruption of Redoubt Volcano, Alaska--highlighting the importance of particle aggregation: Journal of Volcanology and Geothermal Research. doi http://dx.doi.org/10.1016/j.jvolgeores.2012.09.015.

Wilson, L., and Huang, T.C., 1979, The influence of shape on the atmospheric settling velocity of volcanic ash particles: Earth and Planetary Science Letters, v. 44, p. 311-324.

Appendix: Example Ash3d input file

```
#The following is an input file to the model Ash3d,
#Created by L.G. Mastin and R. P. Denlinger, U.S. Geological Survey
#
#GENERAL SOURCE PARAMETERS. DO NOT DELETE ANY LINES
#  LINE 1 of this block gives the volcano name or CAVW number.
#      If the CAVW number is given, Ash3d looks up the default eruption source
#          parameters for this volcano in the ESP table of Mastin (2009, USGS
#          Open-File Report 2009-1133)
#  LINE 2 of this block identifies the projection used and the form of
#          the input coordinates and is of the following format:
#        latlonflag projflag (variable list of projection parameters)
#    projflag should describe the projection used for both the windfile(s) and
#    the input coordinates.  Currently, these need to be the same projection.
#    For a particular projflag, additional values are read defining the projection.
#    latlonflag = 0 if the input coordinates are already projected
#               = 1 if the input coordinates are in lat/lon
#    projflag   = 1 -- polar stereographic projection
#          lambda0 -- longitude of projection point
#          phi0    -- latitude of projection point
#          k0      -- scale factor at projection point
#          radius  -- earth radius for spherical earth
#             = 2 -- Alberts Equal Area
#          lambda0 --
#          phi0    --
#          phi1    --
#          phi2    --
#             = 3 -- UTM
#          zone    -- zone number
#          north   -- flag indication norther (1) or southern (0) hemisphere
#             = 4 -- Lambert conformal conic
#          lambda0 -- longitude of origin
#            phi0 -- latitude of origin
#            phi1 -- latitude of secant1
#            phi2 -- latitude of secant2
#          radius -- earth radius for a spherical earth
#  LINE 5 gives the vent location.  It can take either two or three variables
#      If two variables are given, they are taken to be x and y of the vent
#      If three are given, the third is taken to be vent elevation.  If no
#          vent elevation is given, Ash3d uses the elevation of the topography
#          at this location (or zero, if topography is not used).
#  LINE 8 gives the diffusion coefficient and a parameter determining the
#          vertical distribution of mass.  The vertical distribution may be
#          specified by:
#      A numerical value for the Suzuki constant, assuming that the Suzuki
#          equation is used to specify the vertical distribution of ash in
#          the column of nodes above the volcano.
#      The word 'point'  if all ash is to be concentrated in a single cell at
#          the plume top.
#      The word 'line' if ash is to be distributed evenly in the column of
#          nodes from the ground surface to the plume top.
****************** BLOCK 1 ********************************************
```

```
Redoubt                                  #Volcano name (character*30) or IAVW number
0 1 -135.0 90.0 0.933 6371.229 #Proj flags and params
-1454.327 -3482.752             #x, y of LL corner of grid (km, or deg. if latlonflag=1)
1000.0   1000.0                #grid width and height (km, or deg. if latlonflag=1)
-954.327 -2982.752             #vent location         (km, or deg. if latlonflag=1)
20.0       20.0                #DX, DY of grid cells  (km, or deg.)
1.000                          #DZ of grid cells      (always km)
000.       4.                  #diffusion coefficient (m2/s), Suzuki constant
1                              #neruptions, number of eruptions or pulses
***************************************************************************
#ERUPTION LINES (number = neruptions)
#In the following line, each line represents one eruptive pulse.
#Parameters are (1) start time (yyyy mm dd h.hh (UT)); (2) duration (hrs);
#              (3) plume height;                       (4) eruped volume (km3)
#If the year is 0, then the model run in forecast mode where mm dd h.hh are
#interpreted as the time after the start of the windfile.
#Furthermore, if the duration, plume height or erupted volume is negative, it
#   is replaced with ESP value for that volcano.
****************** BLOCK 2 ***********************************************
0 0 0 1.0   0.25  15.0   0.0018
***************************************************************************
#WIND OPTIONS
#Line 1:  iwind, iwindFormat.  Ash3d will read from either a single 1-D wind
#         sounding, or gridded, time-dependent 3-D wind data, depending on
#         the value of the parameter iwind.
#   For iwind = 1, read from a 1-D wind sounding
#              2, read from 3D gridded ASCII files generated by the Java script
#                 ReadNAM216forAsh3d or analogous.
#              3, read directly from a single NetCDF file.
#              4, read directly from multiple NetCDF files.
#   The parameter iwindFormat specifies the format of the wind files, as follows:
#     iwindFormat =  1: ASCII files (this is redundant with iwind=2
#                    2: NAM_216pw 45km files (provided by Peter Webley)
#                    3: NARR_221 32km (see http://dss.ucar.edu/pub/narr)
#                    4:   unassigned
#                    5: NAM_216 files from idd.unidata.ucar.edu
#                    6: AWIPS_105 90km from idd.unidata.ucar.edu
#                    7: CONUS_212 40km from idd.unidata.ucar.edu
#                    8: NAM_218 12km
#                    9:   unassigned
#                   10: NAM_242 11km http://motherlode.ucar.edu/
#                   20: NCEP GFS 0.5 degree files
#                          (http://www.nco.ncep.noaa.gov/pmb/products/gfs/)
#                   21: ECMWF 0.25deg for Hekla intermodel comparison
#                   22: NCEP GFS 2.5 degree files
#                   23: NCEP DOE Reanalysis 2.5 degree files
#                          (http://dss.ucar.edu/pub/reanalysis2)
#                   24: NASA MERRA
#                   25: NOAA/NCAR Global Reanalysis 1
#                        http://www.esrl.noaa.gov/psd/data/gridded/data.nmc.reanalysis.html
#Line 2:  iHeightHandler. Many plumes extend  higher than the maximum height
#         of numerical weather prediction models. Ash3d handles this as
#         determined by the parameter iHeightHandler, as follows:
#     iHeightHandler = 1, stop the program if the plume height exceeds mesoscale height
```

```
#                       2, wind velocity at levels above the highest node
#                          equal that of the highest node.  Temperatures in the
#                          upper nodes don't change between 11 and 20 km; above
#                          20 km they increase by 2 C/km, as in the Standard
#                          atmosphere.  A warning is written to the log file.
****************** BLOCK 3 ***************************************************
3  10                   #iwind, iwindFormat
2                       #iHeightHandler
10                      #Simulation time in hours
yes                     #stop computation when 99% of erupted mass has deposited?
1                       #nWindFiles, number of gridded wind files (used if iwind>1)
****************************************************************************
#OUTPUT OPTIONS:
#Lines 1-15 require "yes" or "no" indicating whether a particular file type is
#           to be written out.  The file types are given in the comments on
#           each line.
#Line 16 indicates the type of 3-D ash concentration file to write, and is
#           used only if 'yes' is given in line 15.  The options here are
#           'ascii', 'binary', or 'netcdf'.
#Line 17: nWriteTimes   = the number of times output are to be written out
#           to the kml, ascii, or 3-D ash concentration files.   Data
#           may be written out at uneven intervals (e.g. 0.2, 3, 3.4, and
#           12 hours after the eruption start) or at even intervals
#           (e.g. every two hours, starting 2 hours after the eruption start).
#     if nWriteTimes>0, the following line contains nWriteTimes
#               numbers specifying the times of output, in hours after the
#               eruption start.
#     if =-1, write times are assumed to be at even intervals.  The time
#               interval in hours is given by a single number on the
#               following line.
#Line 18: WriteTimes    = Hours between output (if nWritetimes=-1), or
#           times (hours since start of first eruption) for each output
#           (if nWriteTimes >1)
****************** BLOCK 4 ***************************************************
yes     #Write out ESRI ASCII file of final deposit thickness?
yes     #Write out          KML file of final deposit thickness?
yes     #Write out ESRI ASCII deposit files at specified times?
yes     #Write out          KML deposit files at specified times?
yes     #Write out ESRI ASCII files of ash-cloud concentration?
yes     #Write out          KML files of ash-cloud concentration?
yes     #Write out ESRI ASCII files of ash-cloud height?
yes     #Write out          KML files of ash-cloud height?
yes     #Write out          ASCII files of ash-cloud load (T/km2) at specified times?
yes     #Write out          KML files of ash-cloud load (T/km2) at specified times?
yes     #Write ASCII file of deposit arrival times?
yes     #Write KML file of deposit arrival times?
yes     #write ASCII file of cloud arrival times?
yes     #Write KML file of cloud arrival times?
yes     #Write out 3-D ash concentration at specified times?
netcdf  #format of ash concentration files         ('ascii', 'binary', or 'netcdf')
-1      #nWriteTimes
2       #WriteTimes (hours)
****************************************************************************
#WIND INPUT FILES
```

```
#The following block of data contains names of wind files.  The number of
#     lines in this block should equal nWindFiles as given in Block 3, line 5.
#     NOTE:  If iWindFormat=25 in Block 3, line 1, then nWindFiles
#     should equal 1, and Block 5 should contain a single line giving
#     the path of the directory containing NCEP/NCAR Reanalysis files.
#     Subdirectories within this directory should be named by year.
****************** BLOCK 5 *********************************************
Wind_nc/latest.nc
**********************************************************************
#AIRPORT LOCATION FILE
#Lines 1-3 require 'yes' or 'no' indicating whether you would like to write out:
#     Line 1:   an ASCII file listing the arrival time of ash at airports or
#               other locations listed in an airports file
#     Line 2:   a listing of Grain-size distributions in the ASCII file of
#               ash arrival times at airports or other locations
#     Line 3:   a kml file indicating the airports or other locations impacted
#               by ash, along with ash arrival times at those places
#     Line 4:   The name of the file containing airports & other locations of
#               interest.
#     Line 5:   whether to convert coordinates given in the airports file from
#               lat/lon to projected coordinates. (This option is no longer used:
#               coordinates in airport files are now assumed always to be in
#               latitude/longitude).
****************** BLOCK 6 *********************************************
yes                 #Write out ash arrival times at specified locations to ASCII FILE?
no                  #Write out grain-size distribution to ASCII airports file?
yes                 #Write out ash arrival times to kml file?
GlobalAirports.txt  #Name of file containing aiport or other locations
yes                 #Have Proj4 calculate projected coordinates?
**********************************************************************
#GRAIN SIZE GROUPS
#Line 1 contains an integer (nsize) that gives the number of size bins or
#        settling velocity groups.  An optional second parameter (FV_ID)
#        may specify the fall model used.  If no second parameter is given,
#        FV_ID=1 and the fall  model of Wilson and Huang (1979, EPSL v.
#        44, pp. 311-324) is used, with a shape factor f=0.55 which is the
#        average of values measured by them.  Other options for FV_ID are:
#           2  Wilson and Huang fall model with Cunningham Slip factor
#           3  W & H modification of Ganser (1993, Poder Tech., 77:143-152)
#           4  W & H modification of Pfeiffer et al. (2005, JVGR 140:273-294)
#           5  Stokes flow for spheres with Cunningham slip
#Subsequent lines: there should be by nsize lines.  If those lines contain:
#     2  numbers, Ash3d interprets them to be the mass fraction of particles in
#                 that bin, and the settling velocity.  It then calculates fall
#                 assuming a constant settling velocity regardless of elevation.
#     3  numbers, Ash3d interprets them to be:
#                 --size (mm) in that bin
#                 --mass fraction in that bin
#                 --density of particles (kg/m3) in that bin.
#                 Ash3d calculates the settling velocity of each grain size as a
#                 function of elevation using the formula of Wilson and Huang
#                 (1979, EPSL, 44:311-324), assuming the particles have a shape
#                 factor of f=0.44, which is the average of particles measured
#                 by Wilson and Huang.  This calculation also includes a slip
```

```
#                    factor for small particles.
#     4 numbers, Ash3d interprets the first three as before.  The fourth number
#                is assumed to be the shape factor f, defined by Wilson and
#                Huang as (b+c)/2a, where a, b, and c are the semimajor, inter-
#                mediate, and semiminor axes of an ellipsoid.
****************** BLOCK 7 *************************************************
9                           #Number of settling velocity groups
16.00000    0.0521261 800.0  #Grain size (mm), mass fraction, and density (kg/m3)
8.000000    0.0701093 800.0
4.00000     0.0739961 800.0
2.00000     0.0689340 800.0
1.00000     0.1516470 800.0
0.50000     0.1830613 1000.0
0.25000     0.1554387 1083.0
0.12500     0.2060758 1790.6
0.06250     0.0386144 2000.0
*************************************************************************
#Options for writing vertical profiles
#The first line below gives the number of locations (nlocs) where vertical
# profiles are to be written.  That is followed by nlocs lines, each of which
#contain the location, in the same coordinate system specified above for the
#volcano.
****************** BLOCK 8 *************************************************
0                           #number of locations for vertical profiles (nlocs)
*************************************************************************
#netCDF output options
#     Line 1: Name of the output file containing 3-D cloud structure
#     Line 2: Title of this simulation as written in NetCDF 3-D output file
#     Line 3: Optional comment for NetCDF 3-D output file
#     Line 4: Indicates whether topography is to be used ("yes" or "no")
#     Line 5: the first parameter is the topofile format.  This equals 1 if
#             GTOPO30 topography is used (i.e. if the etopo.nc file is used,
#             or 2 if the GEBCO_08.nc topography file is used.
#             The second parameter gives smoothing length, in kilometers.
#             Increasing the smoothing length decreases the number of
#             spurious points in the deposit created by abrupt topography.
#             Smoothing lengths of 30-50 km have yielded reasonable results.
#     Line 6: Topofile name.  This may be either "etopo.nc" (if GTOPO30
#             topography is used), or GEBCO_08.nc, if using the GEBCO topography
#             database.
****************** BLOCK 9 *************************************************
3d_tephra_fall.nc           # Name of output file
Redoubt forecast            # Title of simulation
no comment                  # Comment written to NetCDF file
no                          # use topography?
1 20.                       # Topofile format, smoothing length
etopo.nc                    # topofile name
```